ALFRED's
BEGINNING
WORKBOOK
FOR
DRUM

A Comprehensive Accompaniment for Any Beginning Snare Drum Method

By Nate Brown

Alfred Music Publishing Co., Inc.
16320 Roscoe Blvd., Suite 100
P.O. Box 10003
Van Nuys, CA 91410-0003

Alfred

alfred.com

Contents

WARM UP & RUDIMENT CHART

Practice all checked warm ups & rudiments before working on your lessons.

✓ ADD TO LIST	WARM UP / RUDIMENT	✓ ADD TO LIST	WARM UP / RUDIMENT
	(p.7) Eight on a Hand (Warm Up)		(p.47) Five-Stroke Roll
	(p.7) Three on a Hand (Warm Up)		(p.50) Nine-Stroke Roll
	(p.7) Double-Stroke Roll		(p.55) 13- & 17-Stroke Rolls
	(p.7) Single-Stroke Roll		(p.61) Seven-Stroke Roll
	(p.28) Paradiddle		(p.64) The Flam
	(p.43) Double Paradiddle		(p.66) The Drag

LESSON CHART

Use the chart below to keep track of your lessons and progress.

DATE ASSIGNED	LESSON		✓ COMPLETED
	(p.8) Wholes, Quarters, and Halves	LESSON 1.1	
	(p.9) Quarter Rests	LESSON 1.2	
	(p.10) First Snare Drum Etudes	LESSON 1.3	
	(p.11) Whole Rests and Half Rests 1	LESSON 2.1	
	(p.12) Whole Rests and Half Rests 2	LESSON 2.2	
	(p.13) Eighth Notes 1	LESSON 3.1	
	(p.14) Eighth Notes 2	LESSON 3.2	
	(p.15) Repeats and 1st & 2nd Endings	LESSON 3.3	
	(p.16) Dynamics 1	LESSON 3.4	
	(p.17) Eighth Rests 1	LESSON 4.1	
	(p.18) Eighth Rests 2	LESSON 4.2	
	(p.19) Eighth Notes & Eighth Rests—Duet	LESSON 4.3	
	(p.20) Dotted Half & Dotted Quarter Notes 1	LESSON 5.1	
	(p.21) Dotted Half & Dotted Quarter Notes 2	LESSON 5.2	
	(p.22) Dynamics 2	LESSON 5.3	
	(p.23) Dal Segno al Fine	LESSON 5.4	
	(p.24) Sixteenth Notes	LESSON 6.1	
	(p.25) Sixteenth Notes—Duet	LESSON 6.2	
	(p.26) Eighths Beamed with Sixteenths 1	LESSON 7.1	
	(p.27) Eighths Beamed with Sixteenths 2	LESSON 7.2	
	(p.28) Intro to Rudiments—Paradiddle	LESSON 7.3	
	(p.29) Dynamics 3	LESSON 7.4	
	(p.30) Eighth Rests and Sixteenth Notes	LESSON 8.1	
	(p.31) Improvisation	LESSON 8.2	
	(p.32) Sixteenth Rests	LESSON 8.3	
	(p.33) Check-Up	LESSON 8.4	
	(p.34) Da Capo al Coda	LESSON 8.5	

LESSON CHART (continued)

DATE ASSIGNED	LESSON		✓ COMPLETED
	(p.35) Dotted Eighth Notes 1	LESSON 9.1	
	(p.36) Dotted Eighth Notes 2	LESSON 9.2	
	(p.37) Check-Up	LESSON 9.3	
	(p.38) Time Signatures—Introduction	LESSON 10.1	
	(p.39) $\frac{2}{4}$ Time Signature 1	LESSON 10.2	
	(p.40) $\frac{2}{4}$ Time Signature 2	LESSON 10.3	
	(p.41) $\frac{2}{4}$ Time Signature 3	LESSON 10.4	
	(p.42) $\frac{3}{4}$ Time Signature 1	LESSON 11.1	
	(p.43) Rudiment—Double Paradiddle	LESSON 11.2	
	(p.44) $\frac{3}{4}$ Time Signature 2	LESSON 11.3	
	(p.45) Multiple-Bounce Roll (Closed Roll)	LESSON 12.1	
	(p.46) Double-Stroke Roll (Open Roll)	LESSON 12.2	
	(p.47) The Five-Stroke Roll 1	LESSON 12.3	
	(p.48) The Five-Stroke Roll 2	LESSON 12.4	
	(p.49) The Five-Stroke Roll 3	LESSON 12.5	
	(p.50) The Nine-Stroke Roll 1	LESSON 13.1	
	(p.51) The Nine-Stroke Roll 2	LESSON 13.2	
	(p.52) Five-Stroke Roll & Nine-Stroke Roll	LESSON 13.3	
	(p.53) Five-Stroke & Nine-Stroke Roll—Duet	LESSON 13.4	
	(p.54) Check-Up	LESSON 13.5	
	(p.55) The 13-Stroke Roll & 17-Stroke Roll 1	LESSON 14.1	
	(p.56) The 13-Stroke Roll & 17-Stroke Roll 2	LESSON 14.2	
	(p.57) Eighth-Note Triplets 1	LESSON 15.1	
	(p.58) Eighth-Note Triplets 2	LESSON 15.2	
	(p.59) Sixteenth-Note Triplets 1	LESSON 16.1	
	(p.60) Sixteenth-Note Triplets 2	LESSON 16.2	
	(p.61) The Seven-Stroke Roll 1	LESSON 17.1	
	(p.62) The Seven-Stroke Roll 2	LESSON 17.2	
	(p.63) Check-Up	LESSON 17.3	
	(p.64) The Flam 1	LESSON 18.1	
	(p.65) The Flam 2	LESSON 18.2	
	(p.66) The Drag 1	LESSON 19.1	
	(p.67) The Drag 2	LESSON 19.2	
	(p.68) Changes in Tempo	LESSON 19.3	
	(p.69) Final Solo	LESSON 20.1	
	(p.70) Final Test—Part 1	LESSON 20.2	
	(p.71) Final Test—Part 2	LESSON 20.3	
	(p.72) Final Test—Part 3	LESSON 20.4	

INTRODUCTION

There are four core areas that together make the foundation of today's successful drummers: playing, reading, writing and creating. Inspiring students to excel in these four core areas will help them achieve their fullest potential and open many doors of opportunity as professional, working drummers.

Upon completion of this book, students will have been inspired to develop, explore and master the content. Fun-to-play, realistic rhythms fill every lesson, and opportunities to create and write are strategically placed throughout. This is a workbook that will inspire students to develop a more precise style of playing, reading, writing and creating.

HOW TO USE THIS BOOK

THE CHARTS
Included in the front of this book are both a Warm Up and Lesson Chart. Use the charts to keep track of your lessons and progress. The pace at which you complete the assignments depends on your effort and commitment. It is best to work with a qualified drum teacher that will help you to set an appropriate pace for your individual needs.

WRITING ASSIGNMENTS
The more you practice counting, the better you will become. Use the worksheets in this book to help improve your counting skills and overall understanding of the notes' timing. Be sure to do the writing activities with a pencil, as mistakes will be made. Use the answer sheets in the back of the book to check your work.

FINAL TEST
A final test is included to test your knowledge. This is designed to be a "closed-book" test, meaning you shouldn't look through the book to find the answers. If you find you're having difficulty in a specific area, try those lessons over again until they become comfortable.

IMPORTANCE OF COUNTING

Counting is an important learning tool in music. It makes learning a new beat easier and helps a musician to maintain steady time with the rest of the band. Think of counting as the "screwdriver" in your drumming toolbox. Using a coin, a key or a butter knife will eventually get the screw loose, but the screwdriver gets the job done quickly and efficiently. No drumming toolbox is complete without the tool of counting. Remember to count as you play!

WARMING UP

As with any physical activity, warming up before you play should be an important part of your daily routine. Not only will it help to prevent injuries by loosening your muscles and reducing strain, but it will get your mind ready to play as well. A good warm-up session will get you "in the groove" and ready to perform both mentally and physically.

Below are four basic warm-up exercises to help get you started. The more you practice, the better you'll become at playing them. The faster you go, the more difficult the exercises will become. However, don't expect to play a warm-up at full speed the first time you try it. Speed will come with practice and should not be your only goal. Accuracy, and playing the rhythms correctly and evenly, is a must. Speed without accuracy is worth nothing.

DIRECTIONS: Before playing, warm up each day with the following exercises.

Eight on a Hand
Play eight strokes with the right stick and eight with the left. Without pausing in between, play eight more with the right and eight more with the left. Now, stop! Start this exercise slowly and then gradually build up your speed.

R R R R R R R L L L L L L L L R R R R R R R R L L L L L L L L [stop]

Three on a Hand
Play three strokes with the right stick and three with the left. This exercise does not stop after a certain number of times through. Continue playing three strokes with each stick, gradually changing your speed from slow to fast, and back to slow again.

R R R L L L R R R L L L ...

Double-Stroke Roll (Rudiment)
Play two stokes with each stick. As with Three on a Hand, this exercise does not stop after a certain number of times through. Continue playing two strokes with each stick, gradually changing your speed from slow to fast and back to slow again before you stop.

R R L L R R L L ...

Single-Stroke Roll (Rudiment)
Play one stroke with each stick. As with Three on a Hand and the Double-Stroke Roll, this exercise does not stop after a certain number of times through. Continue playing one stroke with each stick, gradually changing your speed from slow to fast and back to slow again before you stop.

R L R L R L ...

✓ Add these exercises to your warm-up chart (p.4)

Introduction to Music Notation

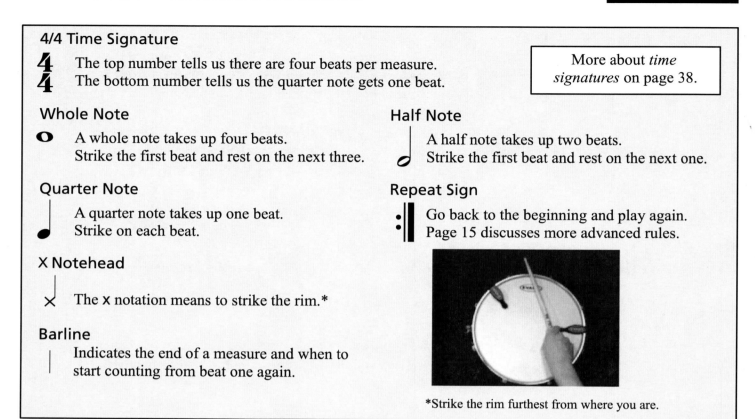

4/4 Time Signature

4/4 The top number tells us there are four beats per measure.
The bottom number tells us the quarter note gets one beat.

More about *time signatures* on page 38.

Whole Note

o A whole note takes up four beats.
Strike the first beat and rest on the next three.

Half Note

A half note takes up two beats.
Strike the first beat and rest on the next one.

Quarter Note

A quarter note takes up one beat.
Strike on each beat.

Repeat Sign

Go back to the beginning and play again.
Page 15 discusses more advanced rules.

X Notehead

X The x notation means to strike the rim.*

Barline

Indicates the end of a measure and when to
start counting from beat one again.

*Strike the rim furthest from where you are.

DIRECTIONS: Write the beat number below each note, and then play each line (see #1).

If you want to succeed, know what you want, be passionate about it, study and work hard —Dave Black, Author & Composer

Quarter Rests

> Quarter Rest
> A quarter rest takes up one beat.
> Count the rest like a quarter note, but do not strike the drum.

PART A

DIRECTIONS: Write the beat number below each note, and then play each line (see #1).

PART B

DIRECTIONS: Draw the bar lines where they belong, write the beat numbers below each note, and then play each line.

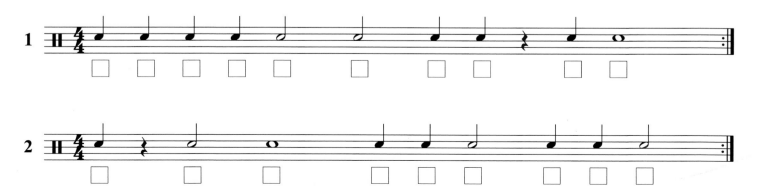

First Snare Drum Etudes

> **End Bar Line**
>
> A thin/thick *bar line* indicates the end of a piece. It looks similar to a repeat but does not have the two dots.

DIRECTIONS: Play the following two pieces.

Close Encounters

Ice Man Groove

*right stick on rim

Whole Rests and Half Rests 1

As the quarter rest is counted like a quarter note, whole notes and half rests are counted like whole notes and half notes. Even though they're counted the same way, remember not to strike the drum on a rest.

Whole Rest
- A whole rest takes up four beats.
  Count the rest like a whole note, but do not strike the drum.

Half Rest
- A half rest takes up two beats.
  Count the rest like a half note, but do not strike the drum.

A trick to remember ...
An easy way to remember which rest is a whole and which is a half is to think of them as a hat. The man is a *whole* gentleman if he takes his hat off all the way in the presence of a lady. He is only *half* a gentleman, however, if he takes it only halfway off.

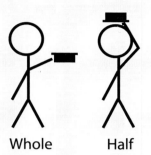

Whole   Half

DIRECTIONS: Draw the bar lines where they belong, and then play each line.

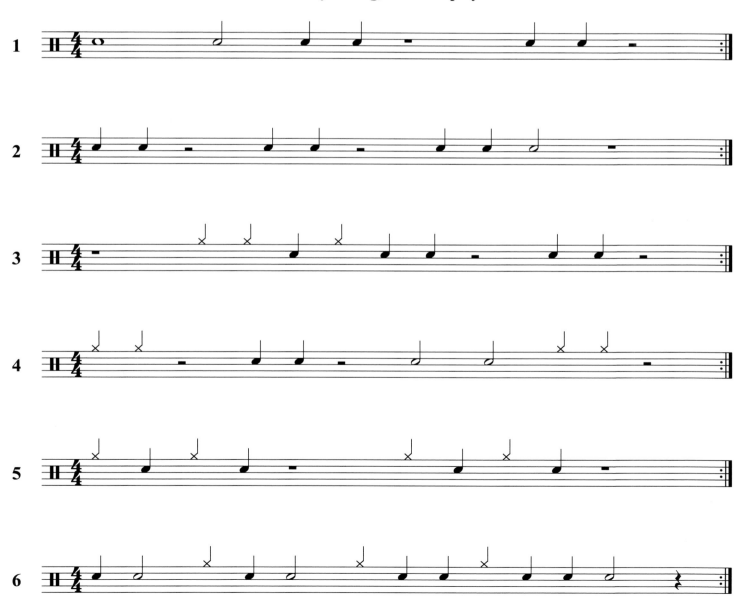

Whole Rests and Half Rests 2

The ability to notate music is another important tool to have in your drumming toolbox. Writing music makes it easier to remember, share and is very useful in creating new drum beats and rhythms.

DIRECTIONS: Write the appropriate note above each number, and the appropriate rest to match each "x" (see #1).

1

2

3

4
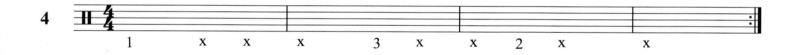

5

6

7

8

Learn the language of music and drumming, and use it to communicate. —JoJo Mayer, Nerve

Eighth Notes 1

The eighth note is one of the most commonly played notes in today's music and, as such, is very important. You will find eighth notes at the heart of almost every hit song. Master the eighth note and you are on your way to becoming a successful drummer.

Eighth Note		Eighth Notes—Beamed	
♪	An eighth note takes up half a beat (two fit in one beat). They are counted "1 & 2 & 3 & 4 &."	♫	When eighth notes are next to each other, their flags can connect to form a *beam*.

DIRECTIONS: Write the beat number below each note using a "+" sign to represent each "&" and then play each line.

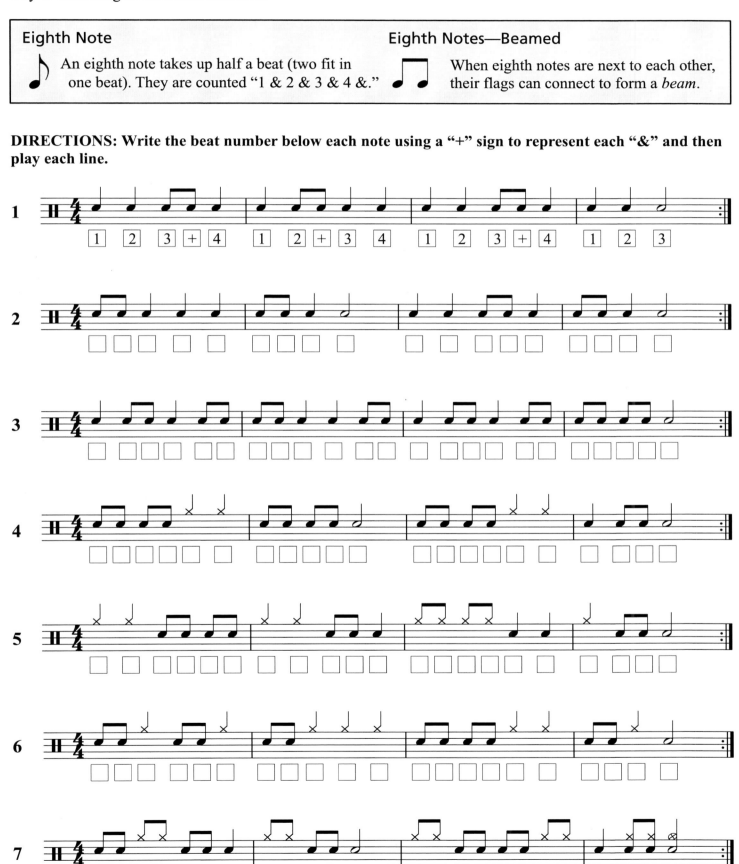

Line 1 beat numbers: 1 2 3 + 4   1 2 + 3 4   1 2 3 + 4   1 2 3

Eighth Notes 2

Which notes should be beamed together?

Most often, notes are beamed together to group them into beats. In other words, all of the notes that make up beat one are beamed together. All of the notes that make up beat two are beamed together. This continues for each beat. However, it is also common to see four eighth notes beamed together, making up two beats. Following a consistent beaming structure makes the music clearer and easier to follow.

PART A

DIRECTIONS: Beam the stems on the notes below so you have the correct number of beats in each measure. Then, write the beat number below each note. There are multiple possibilities for each measure. Be creative!

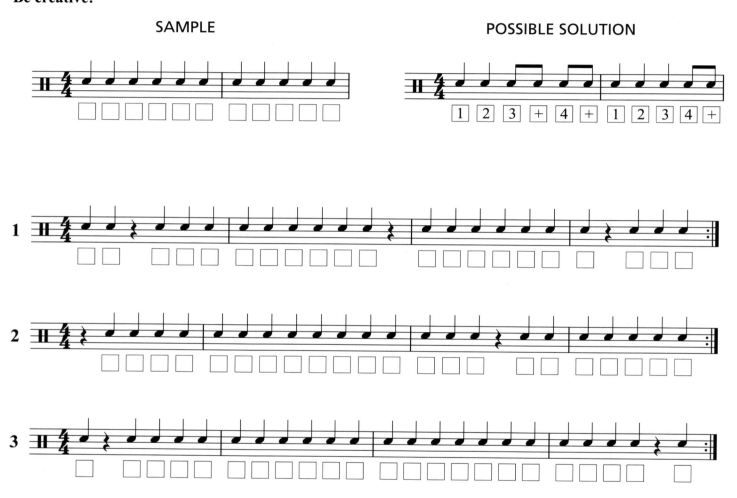

PART B

DIRECTIONS: Complete the measures below with either notes or rests, and then play each line.

Repeats and 1st & 2nd Endings

Repeat Signs

The repeat sign you've used so far is called an *end repeat*. There is another repeat sign called a *start repeat* that looks very similar. It is the mirror image of the *end repeat* with its two dots on the right side (see below).

Start Repeat	End Repeat
Indicates where to start repeating after an *end repeat*. If *a start repeat* is not present, repeat from the beginning of the piece.	Indicates to repeat a selection of music. Once you've repeated the selection, play through the *end repeat* as if it's not there.

DIRECTIONS: Use the following piece to answer the questions below, and then play the piece.

(1) Which measure is played after following the repeat sign in measure 3?   ANSWER: _____

(2) After playing measure 3 the second time, which measure is played?   ANSWER: _____

(3) Which measure is played after following the repeat sign in measure 8?   ANSWER: _____

1st and 2nd Endings

1st and 2nd endings save a lot of space and allow you to repeat a phrase utilizing two different endings. You will come across 1st and 2nd endings very often in your drumming career.

1st Ending	2nd Ending
1.	2.
➜ Play the 1st ending the first time through and repeat the music.	➜ Skip over the 1st ending on the repeat and play the 2nd ending.
	➜ If something comes after the 2nd ending, play it.

DIRECTIONS: Use the piece below to answer the following questions, and then play the piece.

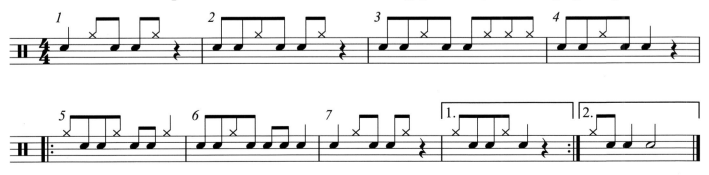

(1) Which measure is played after playing the first ending?   ANSWER: _____

(2) After playing measure 7 for the second time, which ending is played?   ANSWER: _____

Dynamics 1

The term *dynamics* refers to how loudly or softly something is sung or played. Dynamics should already be familiar to you, as we use them in our speech. You may talk loudly when you're angry or softly when you want to keep a secret. Dynamics add meaning and interest to music. A dynamic drummer stands out above the rest.

Piano

p A *piano* marking means to play quietly.
Play *piano* until another dynamic is indicated.

Forte

f A *forte* marking means to play loudly.
Play *forte* until another dynamic is indicated.

Crescendo

Gradually get louder for the notes above the crescendo.

Decrescendo

Gradually get softer for the notes above the decrescendo.

Measure Repeat

A *measure repeat* means to repeat the previous measure and then go on. In other words, whatever you just played, play it again.

PART A

DIRECTIONS: Play the following piece along with the appropriate dynamics.

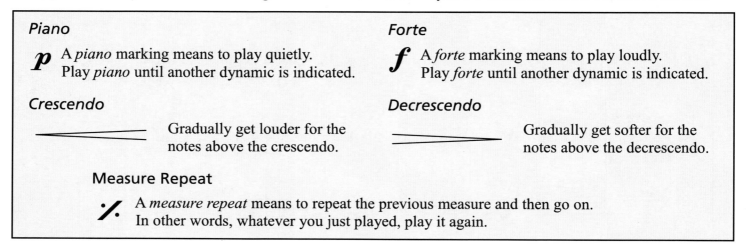

Shank

Turning It Up

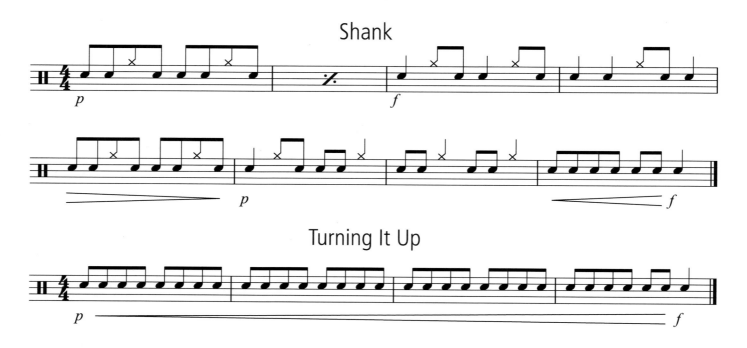

PART B

DIRECTIONS: Add dynamics to the following piece to make it more interesting, and then play the piece.

My Dynamics

You should play from your heart, your soul, your instinct. —Dino Campanella, DREDG

Eighth Rests 1

Eighth Rest	Eighth Note (by itself)
An eighth rest takes up half a beat. Count the rest like an eighth note, but do not strike the drum.	When an eighth note is written by itself, it has a flag on its stem.

DIRECTIONS: Write the beat number below each note, and then play each line.

Eighth Rests 2

PART A

DIRECTIONS: Draw the bar lines where they belong, and write the beat number below each note. The first measure is done for you.

PART B

DIRECTIONS: Write the appropriate note above each number, and the appropriate rest to match each "x" (see measure 1).

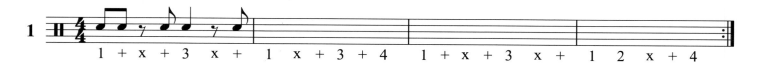

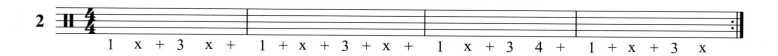

PART C

DIRECTIONS: Add beams and eighth rests to the measures below so you have the correct number of beats in each measure, and then write the beat number below each note.*

SAMPLE   POSSIBLE SOLUTION

*Remember, there are multiple solutions.

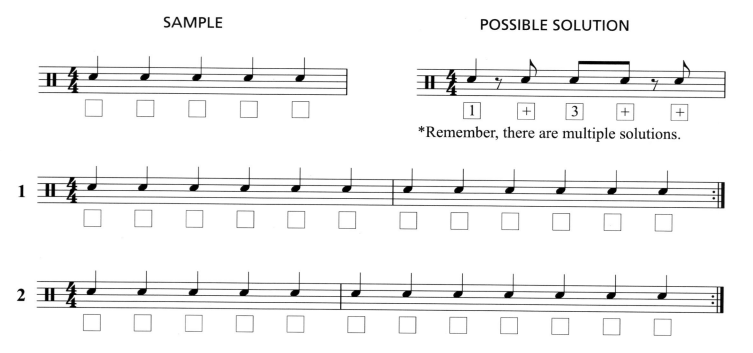

Eighth Notes and Eighth Rests—Duet

A duet is a composition for two performers. In this piece, one drummer will play the first snare drum part, and another drummer will play the second snare drum part. Playing a duet is not only fun, but it helps to build your ability to stay focused on your part in the music.

DIRECTIONS: Play the following duet.

Confidant

I know a lot of dudes that can rip an awesome solo but can't play with other musicians. —Paul Koehler, Silverstein

Dotted Half & Dotted Quarter Notes 1

A dot placed after a note increases the note's value by one-half the value of the original note. For example, the dot after a half note is worth one beat because the half note is worth two (half of two is one). When you add the value of the original half note and the dot, the entire dotted half note is worth three beats.

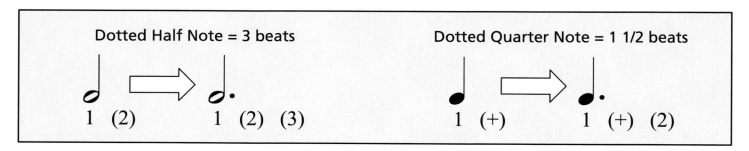

PART A

DIRECTIONS: Write the appropriate beat number in the boxes below, and then play each line (see #1).

PART B

DIRECTIONS: Draw the bar lines where they belong, and then play each line.

Dotted Half & Dotted Quarter Notes 2

PART A

DIRECTIONS: Write the appropriate note above each number, and the appropriate rest to match each "x" (see #1).

1 + x + 3   +   1 + x + 3 x +   1   4 +   1 + x + 3

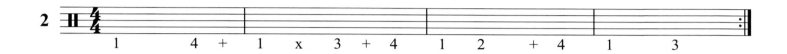

1   4 +   1 x   3 + 4   1   2   + 4   1   3

1   + 3   +   1   + 3 + 4   1 x + 3 x +   1 x + 3   x

PART B

DIRECTIONS: Complete the measures below with the notes and/or rests you've learned so far.

Dynamics 2

So far you have learned four dynamic expressions: *piano, forte, crescendo* and *decrescendo.*
The compositions below incorporate two more dynamic expressions: *pianissimo* and *fortissimo.*

Pianissimo
pp *Pianissimo* means to play very quietly.
Pianissimo is quieter than *piano.*

Fortissimo
ff *Fortissimo* means to play very loudly.
Fortissimo is louder than *forte.*

pp   ***p***   ***f***   ***ff***
very   quiet   loud   very
quiet   loud

PART A

DIRECTIONS: Play the following piece along with the appropriate dynamics.

Short But Sweet

PART B

DIRECTIONS: Add dynamics to the following piece to make it more interesting, and then play the piece.

Pocket

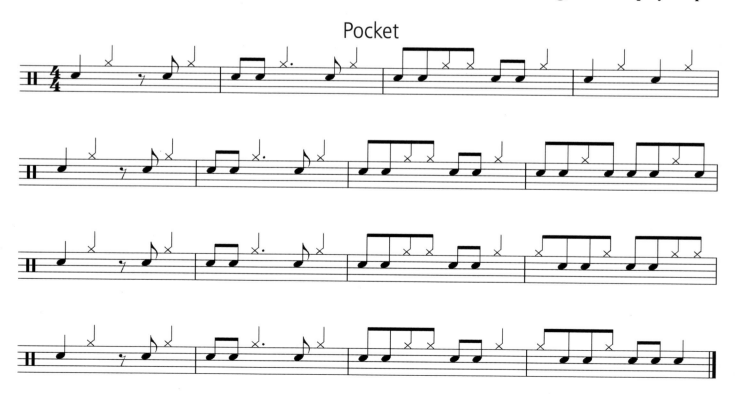

Dal Segno al Fine

> ℅ = The sign. Indicates where to go back after a **D.S.**
>
> **D.S. al Fine** = Go back to *the sign*
>
> *Dal Segno (D.S.)* = Go back to *the sign*
>
> *Fine* = The end

PART A

DIRECTIONS: Use the following piece to answer the questions below, and then play the piece.

Courtside

(1) Which measure is played after playing the second ending?   ANSWER: _____

(2) Which measure is played after playing the first ending?   ANSWER: _____

(3) In which measure does the piece end?   ANSWER: _____

PART B

DIRECTIONS: Add *the sign*, *D.S. al Fine* and *Fine* to the piece below, and then play the piece.

Most successful musicians didn't win their first audition, and if they all quit the first or second time they were turned down, then we wouldn't have Jimi Hendrix, and we wouldn't have all these great players. —Paulo Baldi, CAKE

Sixteenth Notes

Every drummer must master the timing and feel of the sixteenth note. The addition of the sixteenth note will greatly expand your rhythmic possibilities. Used in most of today's popular music, the sixteenth note is another essential tool to add to your drumming "toolbox."

Sixteenth Note

A sixteenth note takes up a quarter (1/4) of a beat. They are counted "1 e & a 2 e & a ..." Four sixteenth notes take up the same amount of time as a quarter note.

Sixteenth Notes Beamed

When sixteenth notes are next to each other, their flags can connect to form two *beams*.

PART A
DIRECTIONS: Write the appropriate beat number in the boxes below, and then play each line (see #1).

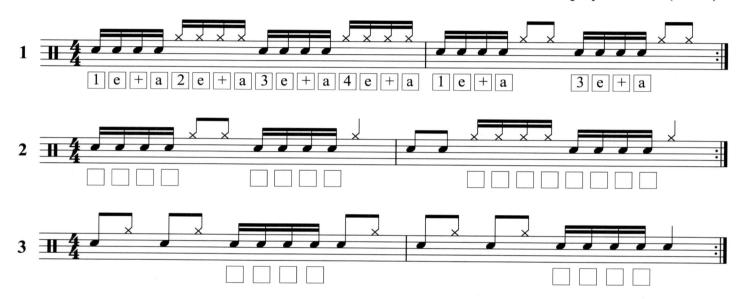

PART B
DIRECTIONS: Add beams to the notes below to make sixteenth and eighth notes that will complete the measure, and then write the beat number below each note.*

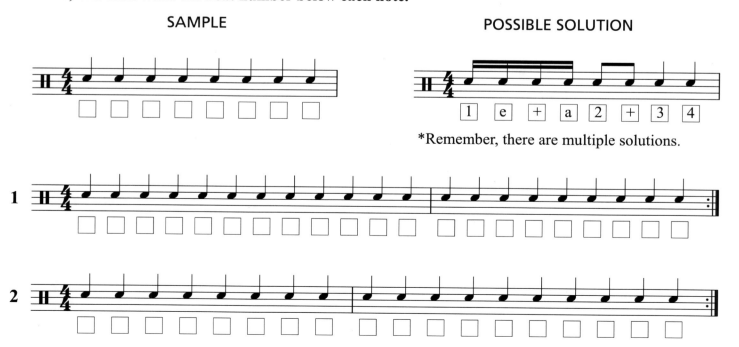

SAMPLE

POSSIBLE SOLUTION

*Remember, there are multiple solutions.

Sixteenth Notes—Duet

DIRECTIONS: Fill in the missing measures to complete the duet, and then add dynamics to the piece.

Your Half

Eighths Beamed with Sixteenths 1

You will often see eighth notes beamed with sixteenth notes. Beaming notes makes them easier to read and makes their rhythmic relationship clearer. Becoming fluent in reading, writing and playing these types of patterns is a must for every drummer.

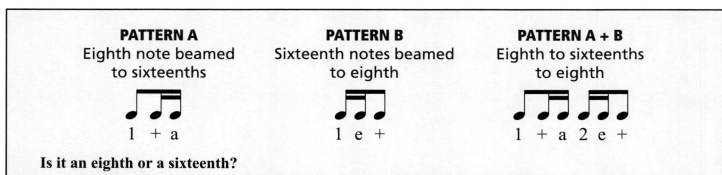

PATTERN A
Eighth note beamed to sixteenths
1 + a

PATTERN B
Sixteenth notes beamed to eighth
1 e +

PATTERN A + B
Eighth to sixteenths to eighth
1 + a 2 e +

Is it an eighth or a sixteenth?
An easy way to tell if a note is an eighth note or a sixteenth note is to look at the number of beams attached to its stem. If there is one beam touching its stem, it's an eighth note. If there are two beams touching its stem, it's a sixteenth note.

DIRECTIONS: Write the beat number below each note, and then play each line.

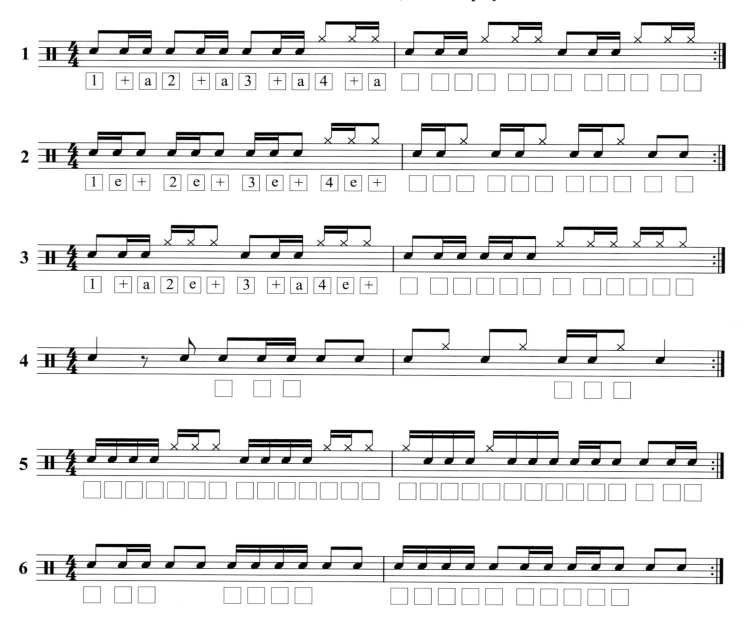

Eighths Beamed with Sixteenths 2

PART A

DIRECTIONS: Write the appropriate note above each number, and the appropriate rest to match each "x."

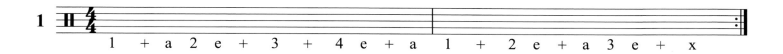

1   1   +   a   2   e   +   3   +   4   e   +   a | 1   +   2   e   +   a   3   e   +   x

2   1   2   e   +   a   3   +   a   4 | 1   +   a   2   e   +   3   +   4

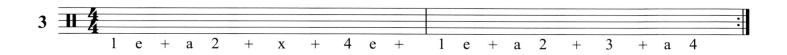

3   1   e   +   a   2   +   x   +   4   e   + | 1   e   +   a   2   +   3   +   a   4

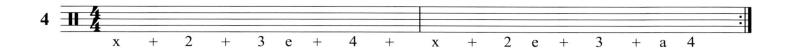

4   x   +   2   +   3   e   +   4   + | x   +   2   e   +   3   +   a   4

PART B

DIRECTIONS: Write your own lines of music using the notes and rests shown below.

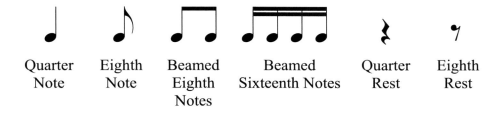

| Quarter Note | Eighth Note | Beamed Eighth Notes | Beamed Sixteenth Notes | Quarter Rest | Eighth Rest |

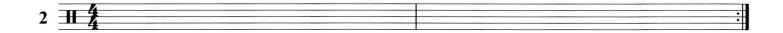

1

2

3

Intro to Rudiments — Paradiddle

As a drummer, you'll often hear the word *rudiment*. Rudiments are the foundation of drumming, and consist of rhythms and sticking patterns used to develop coordination and skill. More importantly, rudiments are the foundation of the rhythms you will play as a drummer. There are 40 snare drum rudiments defined by the Percussive Arts Society. Learning to play rudiments will greatly improve your coordination and technique.

DIRECTIONS: Play the paradiddle below. Notes with an R should be played with the right stick and those with an L with the left. Play the paradiddle variations, and be sure to play the appropriate accents.

Paradiddle

Paradiddle Variations

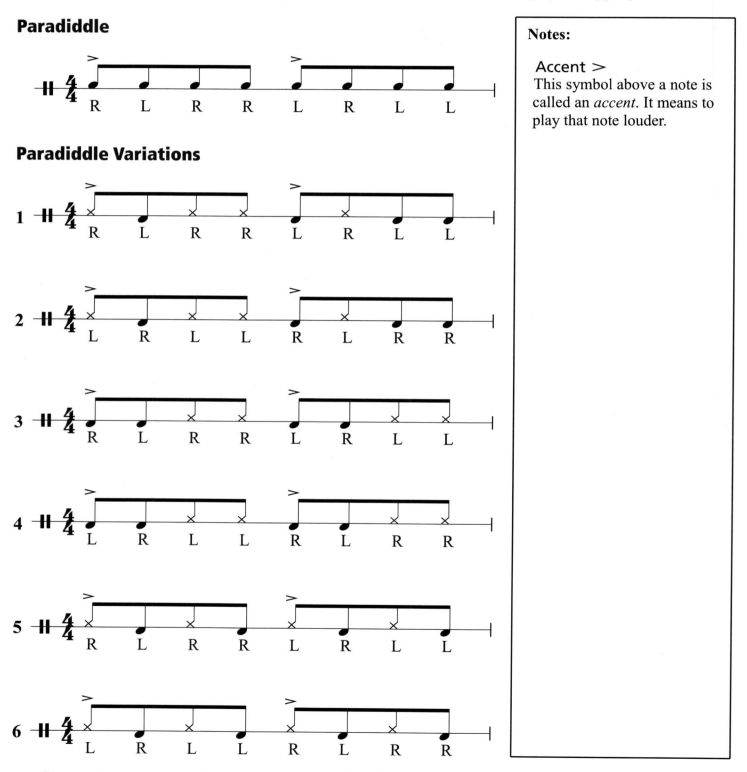

> **Notes:**
>
> Accent >
> This symbol above a note is called an *accent*. It means to play that note louder.

[To expand your musical] vocabulary, you must work on the tools to do so. I think of rudiments as words. You use words to create sentences and paragraphs. You use them to tell a story and, ultimately, say something on the instrument. —Todd Sucherman, STYX

✔ Add these exercises to your Warm-Up Chart (p.4)

Dynamics 3

So far you have learned seven dynamic expressions: *pianissimo, piano, forte, fortissimo, crescendo, decrescendo* and the *accent*. The activities below incorporate two more dynamic expressions: *mezzo-piano* and *mezzo-forte*. The term *mezzo* means *medium*.

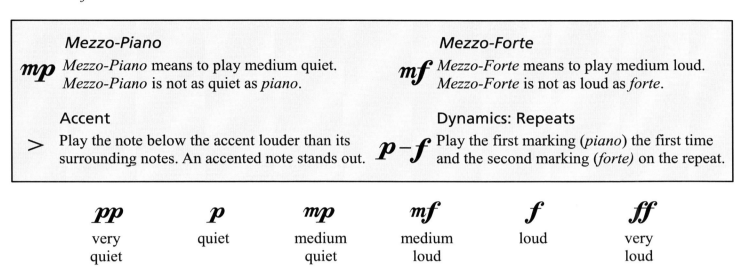

Mezzo-Piano

mp *Mezzo-Piano* means to play medium quiet. *Mezzo-Piano* is not as quiet as *piano*.

Accent

> Play the note below the accent louder than its surrounding notes. An accented note stands out.

Mezzo-Forte

mf *Mezzo-Forte* means to play medium loud. *Mezzo-Forte* is not as loud as *forte*.

Dynamics: Repeats

p–f Play the first marking (*piano*) the first time and the second marking (*forte*) on the repeat.

pp	***p***	***mp***	***mf***	***f***	***ff***
very quiet	quiet	medium quiet	medium loud	loud	very loud

PART A
DIRECTIONS: Play the following piece, and be sure to play the appropriate dynamics.

On the Repeat

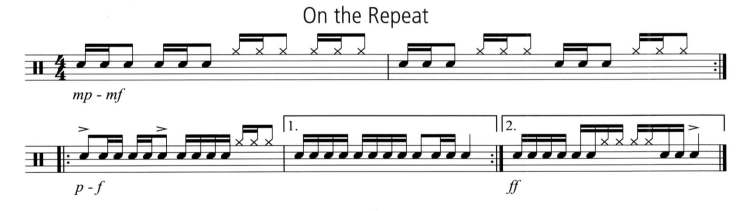

PART B
DIRECTIONS: Add dynamics to the following piece to make it more interesting, and then play the piece.

Hear This

Eighth Rests and Sixteenth Notes

Sixteenth notes are often accompanied by eighth rests, giving the rhythm a syncopated, up-beat feel.
The rhythms are counted the same as Pattern A and Pattern B on page 26, but the eighth note is silent.
Try the rhythms below.

DIRECTIONS: Draw the bar lines where they belong, and then play each line.

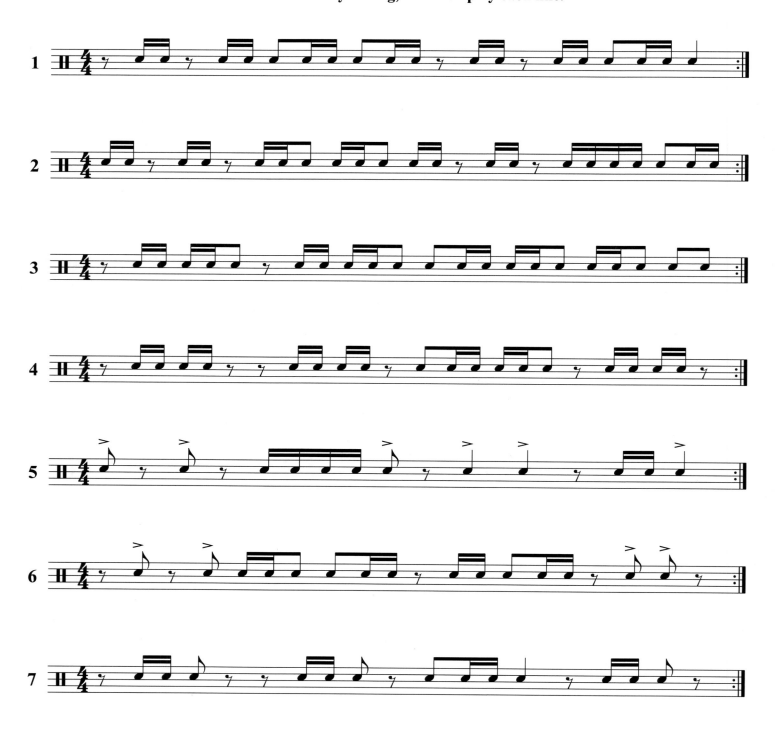

Improvisation

As a working drummer, many of the beats and compositions you play will rely heavily on your improvisational skills. Simply defined, *improvisation* means to make it up as you go. It's important, however, that the beats you make up as you go fit with the general feel of the composition. It needs to flow with the rest of the music. *Improvising* is often referred to as *ad-libbing*. If you see the phrase *ad lib.* (or a slash—see below) in a piece of music, it means to improvise that selection.

> **Slash**
> A slash means to improvise (ad lib.) a selection of music.
> Make sure the beats you play match the general feel of the piece.

DIRECTIONS: Play the following lines, and improvise where indicated.

It is absolutely important for any drummer to find the groove. —Louie Bellson

Sixteenth Rests

> **Sixteenth Rest**
> A sixteenth rest takes up a quarter (1/4) of a beat. Count the rest like a sixteenth note, but do not strike the drum.
>
> **Sixteenth Note**
> When a sixteenth note is written by itself, it includes two flags on its stem.

PART A
DIRECTIONS: Write the appropriate beat number in the boxes below, and then play each line.

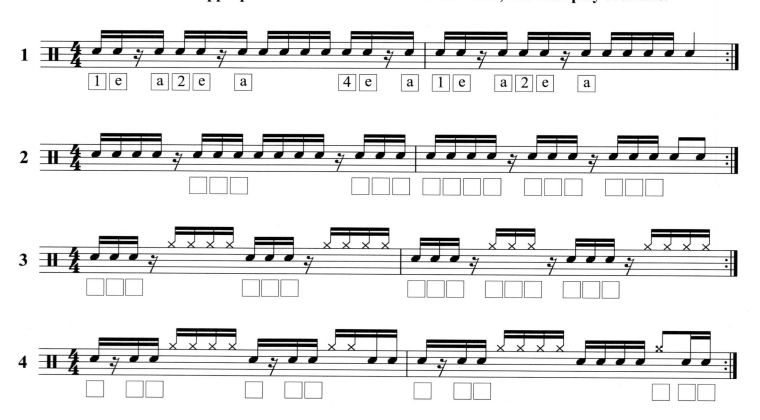

PART B
DIRECTIONS: Add beams and rests to the notes below to make sixteenth and eighth notes/rests that will complete the measure, and then write the beat number below each note.*

SAMPLE

POSSIBLE SOLUTION

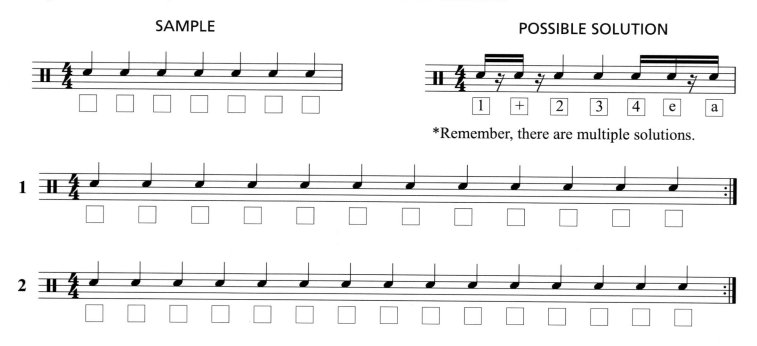

*Remember, there are multiple solutions.

Check-Up

PART A

**DIRECTIONS: In the spaces below, write the total number of beats for each line.
The first one is done for you.**

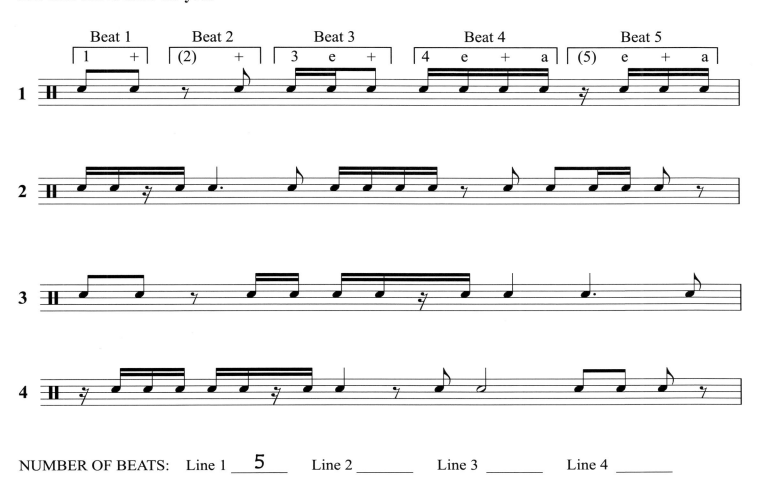

NUMBER OF BEATS: Line 1 ___5___   Line 2 _____   Line 3 _____   Line 4 _____

PART B

**DIRECTIONS: In the boxes below, write the selection from the right that will complete the measure on
the left. In other words, match the selections that together will add up to four beats.**

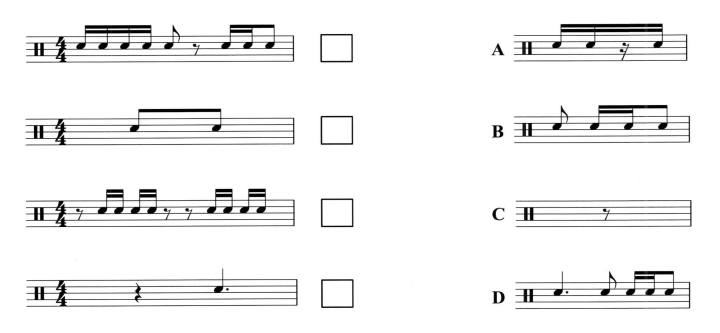

Da Capo al Coda

$\oplus$ = Coda sign

D.C. al Coda = Go back to the beginning and play to the coda sign ($\oplus$). Once you reach the first coda sign, skip ahead to the second coda sign, and play from there.

Da Capo (D.C.) = Go back to the beginning

2 Two-measure repeat. When you see
∙//. this, repeat the previous two measures.

PART A

DIRECTIONS: Use the piece below to answer the questions that follow, and then play the piece.

Shank

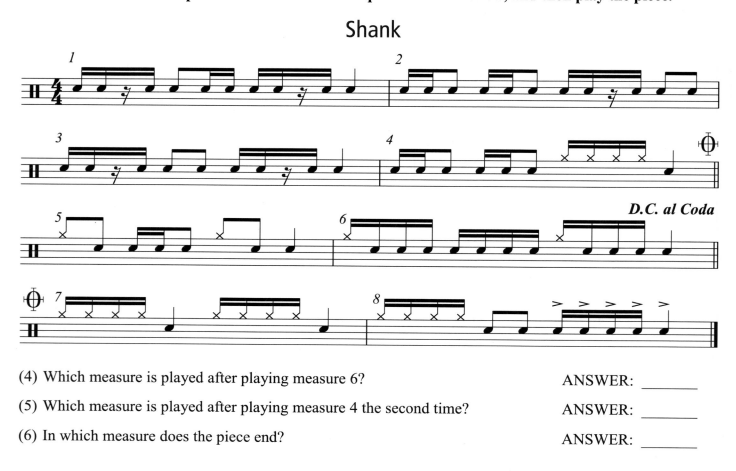

(4) Which measure is played after playing measure 6?   ANSWER: _____

(5) Which measure is played after playing measure 4 the second time?   ANSWER: _____

(6) In which measure does the piece end?   ANSWER: _____

PART B

DIRECTIONS: Add *coda signs* and *D.C. al Coda* to the piece below, and then play the piece.

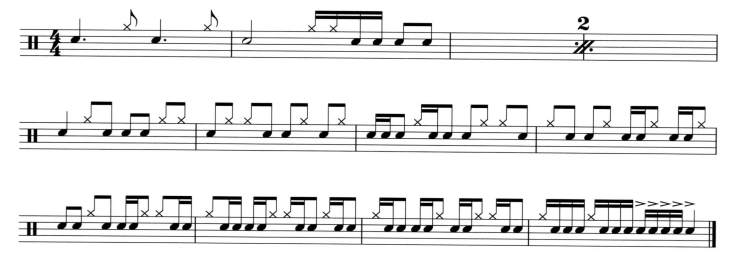

Dotted Eighth Notes 1

Remember that a dot placed after a note increases the note's value by one-half the value of the original note. An eighth note is worth half a beat. Therefore, a dot increases its value by a quarter of a beat (half of a half).

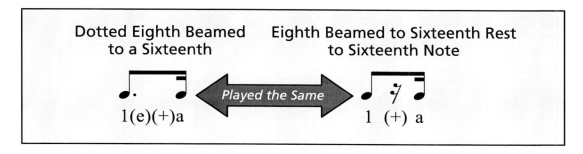

PART A
DIRECTIONS: Write the appropriate beat number in the boxes below, and then play each line.

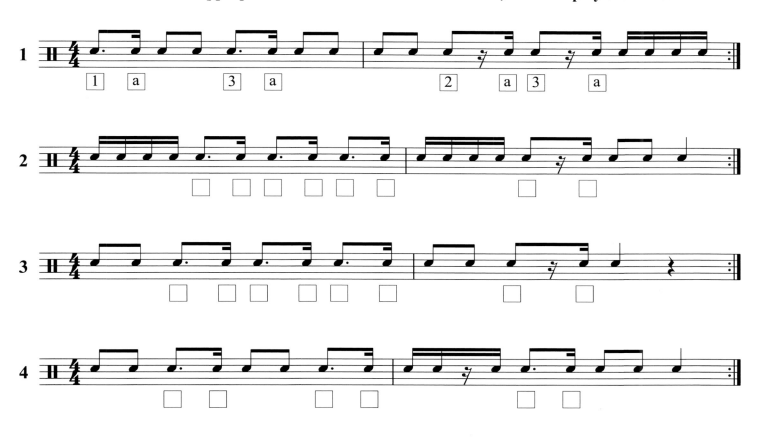

PART B
DIRECTIONS: Complete the measures below with notes and/or rests.

Dotted Eighth Notes 2

Rhythmic Synonyms

Rhythmic synonyms occur when two different notations express the same rhythm. Many of the rhythms you play can be written in multiple ways. The goal of the writer is to choose the best notation to communicate the music to the reader. For example, if a melody in a song is played with eighth notes, but the drummer is to play on the down beats (1, 2, 3, 4), a writer might choose to write the drum part as eighth notes and eighth rests to help communicate the overall picture of the music to the drummer. It's important to be able to read the rhythms any way the writer may choose to communicate them.

DIRECTIONS: Each rhythm on the left matches up with one of the rhythms on the right—they're just notated differently. The first one is done for you.

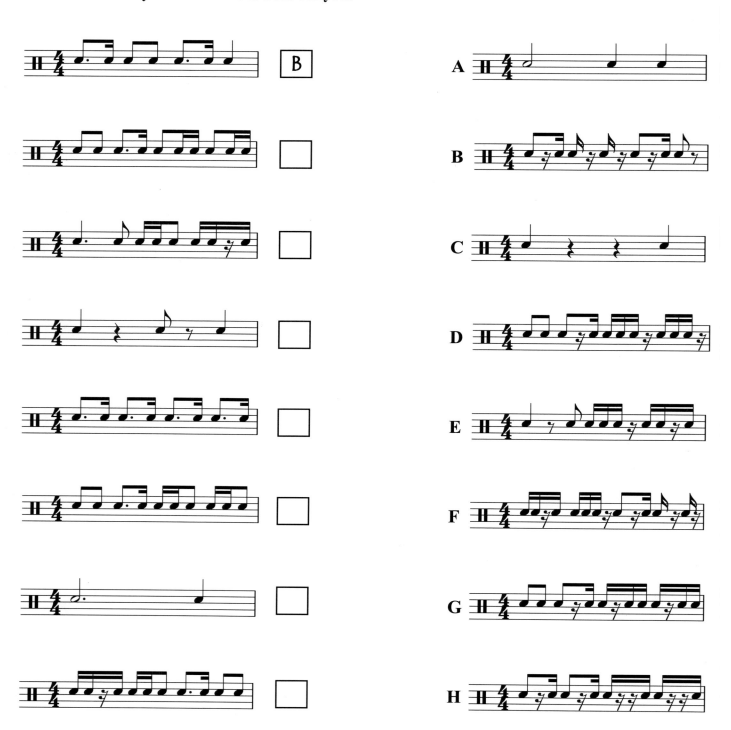

Be tenacious. It's hard sometimes. It's so easy to give up, but don't! —Pat Torpey, Mr. Big

Check-Up

Drumming is a creative art. Often times you will be asked to create your own drum part for a song. You may even be asked to write a drum part for somebody else to play. Similarly, drum solos and breaks are often a personal creation of the drummer. Whatever the situation may be, at some point you will find yourself having to create. The skill of creating is not only an important one but essential to your success as a drummer.

DIRECTIONS: Using the notes and rests pictured below, write your own drum rhythms on the lines provided. Be sure to use dynamics and repeats as you see fit.

Quarter Note	Dotted Quarter	Eighth Note	Beamed Eighth Notes	Beamed Sixteenth Notes	Eighth–Sixteenths Beamed	Sixteenths –Eighth Beamed	Dotted Eighths	Quarter Rest	Eighth Rest	Sixteenth Rest

Time Signatures—Introduction

There are many different time signatures. For a simple explanation, time signatures tell the reader how many beats are in a measure and which notes get a full beat. They don't actually change the sound of a rhythm. The same rhythm can be written in multiple time signatures and still sound exactly the same. Keep in mind that time signatures change the way rhythms are counted, not how they are played.

THE TOP NUMBER

A time signature consists of a top number and a bottom number. The top number indicates the number of beats (counts) in each measure. If a 3 is on top, count three beats per measure. If a 2 is on top, count two beats per measure.

THE BOTTOM NUMBER

The bottom number indicates which kind of note receives one beat. If an 8 is on the bottom, an eighth note will get one beat. If a 2 is on bottom, a half note will get one beat. In this book, we work only with time signatures that have a 4 on the bottom, which means that a quarter note will get one beat. See the examples below.

Example: 4 on the bottom
A 4 on the bottom means a quarter note will get one whole beat. This is what is used in this book.

Example: 8 on the bottom
An 8 on the bottom means an eighth note will get one whole beat.

Example: 2 on the bottom
A 2 on the bottom means a half note will get one whole beat.

Example: 16 on the bottom
A 16 on the bottom means a sixteenth note will get one whole beat.

How do you know which note each bottom number represents?
Here's the trick: think of the number as the bottom number of a fraction with a 1 on top. For example, if 4 is the bottom number, think of the fraction 1 over 4 or 1/4. This fraction is commonly referred to as a *quarter*. Therefore, the 4 represents a quarter note. If an 8 were the bottom number, think of the fraction 1 over 8 or 1/8. This fraction is called an *eighth*. Therefore, an 8 represents an eighth note. See the list below.

List of the most common numbers in a time signature and their meanings

Top Number	Meaning
2	Two beats in a measure
3	Three beats in a measure
4	Four beats in a measure
5	Five beats in a measure

Bottom Number	Meaning
2	Half note gets 1 beat
4	Quarter note gets 1 beat
8	Eighth note gets 1 beat
16	Sixteenth note gets 1 beat

2/4 Time Signature 1

So far you've learned the 4/4 time signature, which is the most common time signature used in today's music. However, there are many times when you'll need to play in other time signatures. Familiarizing yourself and becoming comfortable playing in multiple time signatures is an important step in your development.

> ### 2/4 Time Signature
> **2** The top number tells us there are two beats per measure.
> **4** The bottom number tells us that the quarter note gets one beat.
>
> | More about *time signatures* on page 38. |
>
> ### Notes' Timing ...
> Notes are counted and played the same as the 4/4 time signature. In 2/4, however, instead of counting four beats in each measure, you will only count two beats.

DIRECTIONS: Draw the bar lines where they belong, write the beat number below the notes with boxes, and then play each line.

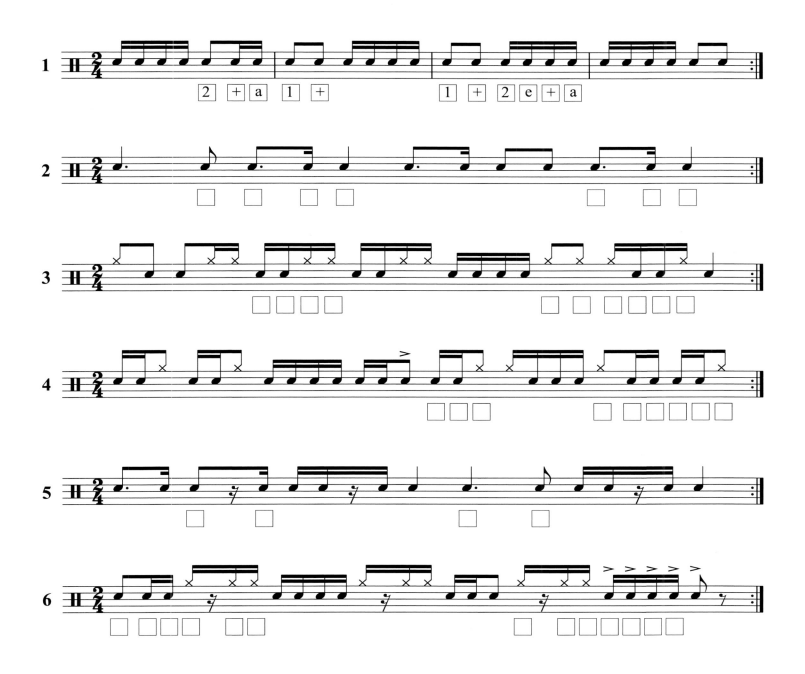

$\frac{2}{4}$ Time Signature 2

PART A

DIRECTIONS: Play the following duet.

Knee High Trail

PART B

DIRECTIONS: Play the following lines and improvise where indicated. Make sure your improvisations fit the general feel of the line.

The song is the most important part of being in a band ... If this thing fits, great.
If it doesn't make the song better, don't do it. —Frank Ferrer, Guns N' Roses

²⁄₄ Time Signature 3

PART A

DIRECTIONS: In the boxes below, write the letter of the selection from the right that will complete the measure on the left. In other words, match the selections that together will add up to two beats. The first one is done for you.

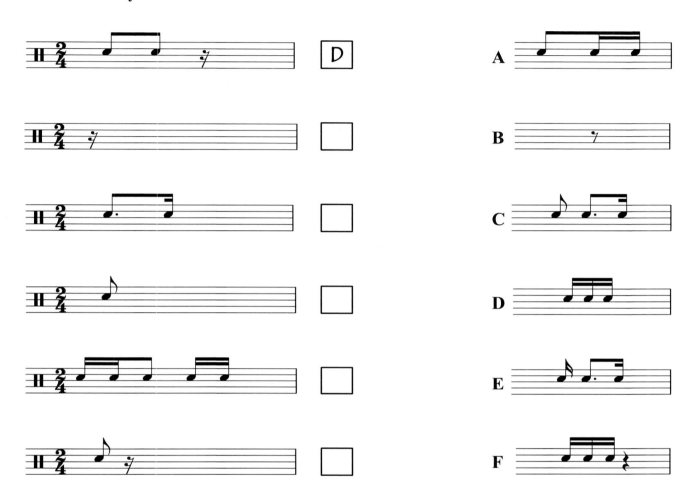

PART B

DIRECTIONS: Complete the measures below with notes and/or rests.

$\frac{3}{4}$ **Time Signature 1**

So far you have learned the $\frac{2}{4}$ and $\frac{4}{4}$ time signatures. Another important time signature is the $\frac{3}{4}$ time signature. Familiarizing yourself and becoming comfortable with multiple time signatures is an important step in becoming a well-rounded drummer.

3/4 Time Signature

$\frac{3}{4}$ The top number tells us there are three beats per measure.
The bottom number tells us that the quarter note gets one beat.

> More about *time signatures* on page 38.

DIRECTIONS: Draw the bar lines where they belong, write the beat number below the notes with boxes, and then play each line (see #1).

Rudiment—Double Paradiddle

Along with the *single paradiddle* (p.28), the *double paradiddle* is also one of the 40 snare drum rudiments defined by the Percussive Arts Society.

DIRECTIONS: Play the double paradiddle below, and then play the variations including the rim (indicated with an "X" notehead). Notes with an R should be played with the right stick and those with an L with the left.

Double Paradiddle

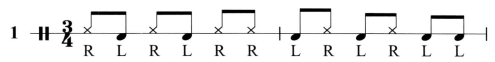

Double Paradiddle Variations

1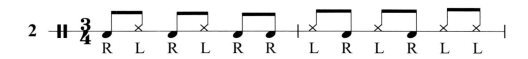

2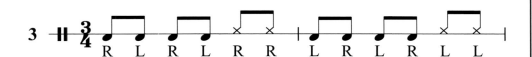

3

4

5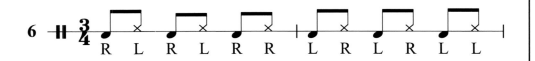

Notes:

Being able to play the rudiments is one thing. Finding nice ways to apply them ... is a completely different matter. —Gavin Harrison, Porcupine Tree

✔ Add these exercises to your Warm-Up Chart (p.4)

¾ **Time Signature 2**

PART A
DIRECTIONS: Play the following piece. Be sure to play the appropriate dynamics, including the accents.

Standing, Not Sitting

PART B
DIRECTIONS: Add dynamics, repeats and/or 1st & 2nd endings to the following piece.
Be sure to include accents to make the piece pop, and then play the piece.

pp	p	mp	mf	f	ff	>
very quiet	quiet	medium quiet	medium loud	loud	very loud	accent

Determination

Multiple-Bounce Roll (Closed Roll)

Another rudiment defined by the Percussive Arts Society is the *multiple-bounce roll*, which is often referred to as the *buzz* or *closed roll*. The goal of the buzz roll is to make a continuous sounding buzz on the drum by playing alternating buzz strokes with the left and right stick (R L R L ...). This roll is most recognized as the one that comes after the announcer says, "and the winner is ... *[buzz roll starts]*." A great-sounding multiple-bounce roll can really define your skill as a drummer.

The Buzz Stroke (for Closed Roll)

In drumming, changing the stroke style gives the drummer a selection of sounds to pick from, even while playing on one surface. One important stroke in drumming is called the buzz stroke. Instead of hitting the drumhead and allowing the stick to freely bounce back, the buzz stroke leaves the tip of the stick on the head in order to produce a buzz sound.

How to play the multiple-bounce roll
Play alternating buzz strokes (R L R L ...) so there are no spaces between each stroke. Adjust the pressure of the stick against the head in order to change the duration of the buzz.

Buzz Stroke
- A **z** on the stem of a note indicates it is a buzz stroke.
- Buzz the note instead of striking as normal.

Learning to "buzz" in 3 steps
1. Strike the drumhead as normal, but instead of letting the stick bounce back, press it into the head.
2. Strike the head, but don't press down as hard as you did in 1 above.
3. The harder you press down, the shorter the buzz you'll get. Find a pressure that gives you a good buzz sound.

DIRECTIONS: Use the exercise below to practice your multiple-bounce roll.

So much of what makes a session good or bad comes down to the work ethic and attitude of the players, in particular the drummer. —Rob Graves, Producer

Double-Stroke Roll (Open Roll)

Another roll rudiment defined by the Percussive Arts Society is the *double-stroke open roll*. The difference between this roll and the multiple-bounce roll (from the previous page) is the stroke type. The double-stroke roll uses what's called *double strokes* to produce a continuous, even-sounding roll. Each hit on the drumhead in a double-stroke roll is clearly heard and played metrically (or in time with the music). A great sounding double-stroke roll can set you apart from other drummers.

The Double Stroke (for Open Rolls)

The goal of this stroke is to produce two hits on the drumhead with one wrist motion, hence the name "double stroke." Achieving the double stroke is similar to the buzz stroke. Like the buzz stroke, instead of hitting the drumhead and allowing the stick to freely bounce back, the double stroke leaves pressure on the tip of the stick to cause the stick to bounce. However, the stick must be stopped or "caught" after it hits twice.

DOUBLE STROKE (Diddle)

- A slash on the stem of a note often indicates a double stroke (or diddle).
- Play a double stroke (two hits) for this note.

Learning to "double stroke" in 3 steps
1. Strike the drumhead as normal, but instead of letting the stick bounce back, press it into the head.
2. Strike the head but don't press it down as hard as you did in 1 above.
3. Apply less and less pressure until you get a clear double bounce (two hits), and then stop the stick with your fingers.

How to play the double-stroke open roll
Play alternating double strokes (RR LL RR LL ...) so each stroke (including the bounces) is evenly spaced and played at the same volume. It's important that every stroke is played in time. A good sounding double stroke should sound the same as alternating single strokes.

DIRECTIONS: Use the exercise below to practice your double-stroke open roll.

The Five-Stroke Roll 1

As rolls are so common, we need a special notation to quickly and clearly communicate the length of the roll. The first roll notation you'll learn is the five-stroke roll. It is executed by playing two buzz or double strokes followed by a single hit. It is called the five-stroke roll because when playing it "open" (with double strokes) there are a total of five strokes on the drumhead. Because the five-stroke roll is short, it can easily be added to a number of rhythms to spice them up.

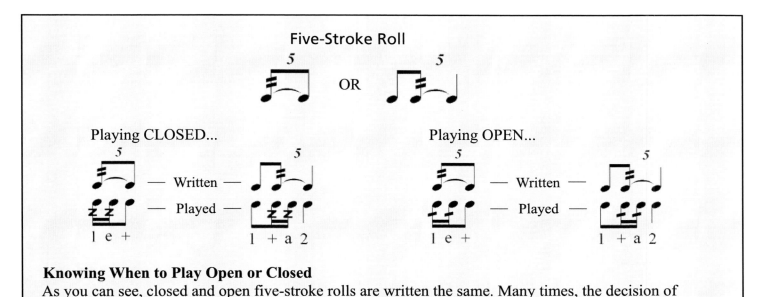

Knowing When to Play Open or Closed

As you can see, closed and open five-stroke rolls are written the same. Many times, the decision of whether to play open (double strokes) or closed (buzz strokes) is up to the drummer, conductor or teacher (classical = buzz; rudimental = open). Look for special instructions in the music or from the director. If it's not indicated, the decision is the drummer's.

DIRECTIONS: Write the appropriate beat numbers in the boxes below, and then play each line. Be sure to note the time signature of each line (see #1).

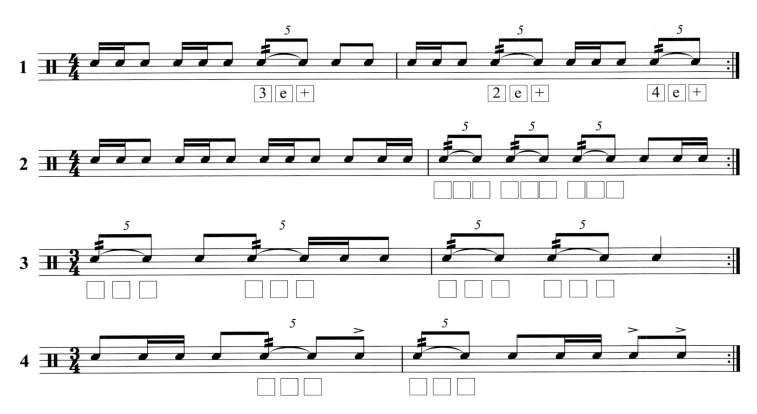

✔ Add the five-stroke roll to the Warm-Up Chart (p.4)

The Five-Stroke Roll 2

DIRECTIONS: For each measure below, complete the top number of the time signature.
Then, write the letter of the measure on the right that is counted the same as the measure on the left.
The first one is done for you.

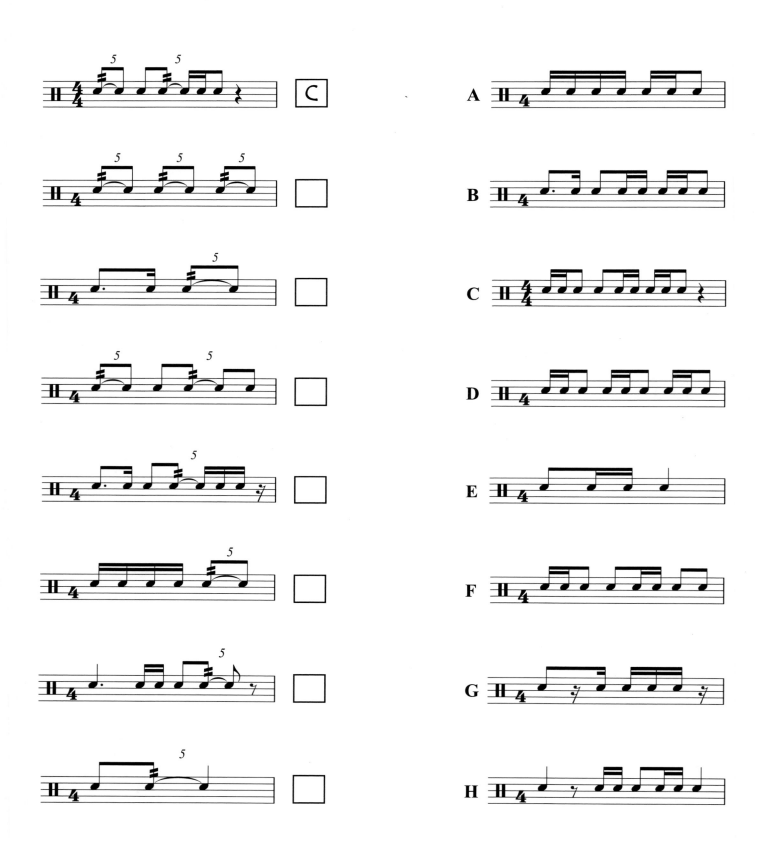

The Five-Stroke Roll 3

PART A

DIRECTIONS: Write the appropriate note above each number, the appropriate rest to match each "x," and rolls where there is an asterisk (*) under the count. The first one is done for you.

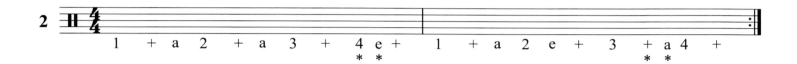

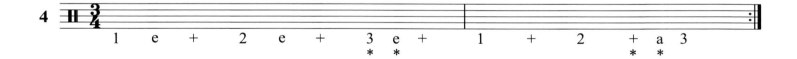

PART B

DIRECTIONS: Complete the measures below with notes and/or rests.
Be sure to look at the time signature.

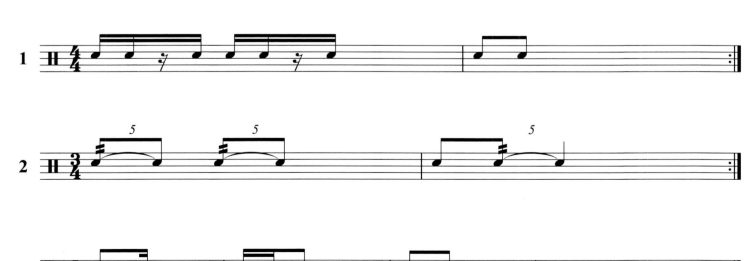

The Nine-Stroke Roll 1

The nine-stroke roll is executed by playing four sets of buzz or double strokes, followed by a single hit. When playing "open" (with double strokes), there are a total of nine strokes played on the drumhead, giving the nine-stroke roll its name.

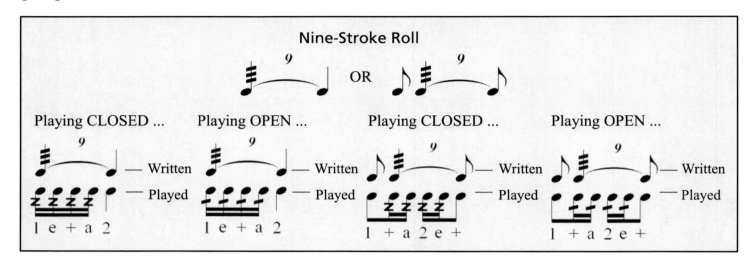

DIRECTIONS: Write the appropriate beat numbers in the boxes below, and then play each line. Be sure to note the time signature of each line. The first one is done for you.

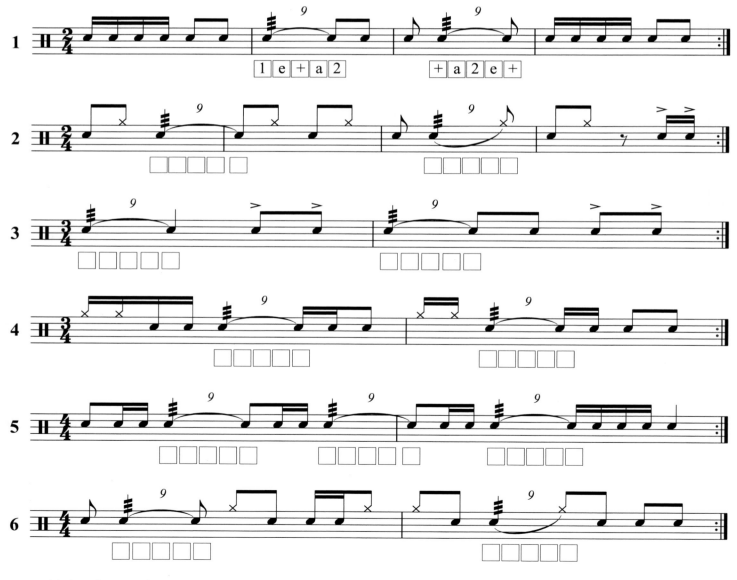

✔ Add the nine-stroke roll to the Warm-Up Chart (p.4)

The Nine-Stroke Roll 2

DIRECTIONS: For each measure below, complete the top number of the time signature, and then write the letter of the measure on the right that is counted the same as the measure on the left. The first one is done for you.

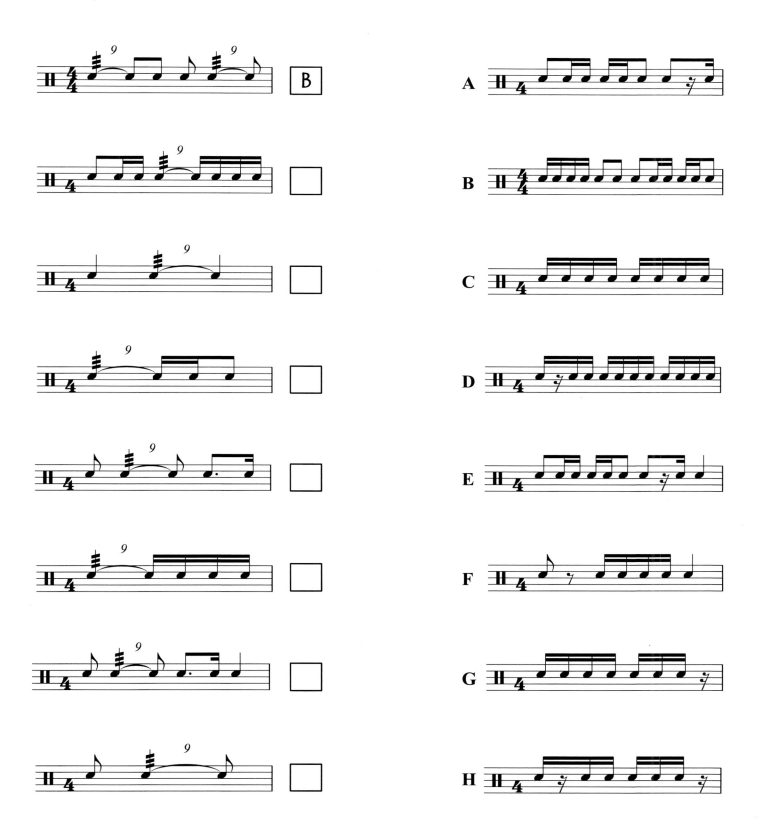

If we all become better drummers, then we all get to share better and better music with the world! —Rich Lackowski, Author

Five-Stroke Roll & Nine-Stroke Roll

DIRECTIONS: Write the appropriate beat numbers in the boxes below, and then play each line. Be sure to note the time signature of each line. The first one is done for you.

Five-Stroke Roll & Nine-Stroke Roll—Duet

DIRECTIONS: Play the following duet.

There It Is

Check-Up

Continue practicing your writing and creative skills by writing six rhythms below. Try not to rush through this. Think about the rhythms by first sounding them out in your head, and by tapping them out before and after you've written them. The more you create, the easier it will become. A drummer that can create great rhythms is an asset to any band.

DIRECTIONS: Write your own lines of music using any of the notes, rests and/or rolls you've learned so far. Take your time, and be creative!

It's good to put yourself out of your element for awhile ... you wind up learning so much more, and then you're able to bring back something new and different to the way you perform or write. —Roy Mayorga, Stone Sour

The 13-Stroke Roll & 17-Stroke Roll 1

13-Stroke Roll

The 13-stroke roll is executed by playing six sets of buzz or double strokes followed by a single hit. When playing "open" (with double strokes), there are a total of 13 strokes played on the drumhead, giving the 13-stroke roll its name.

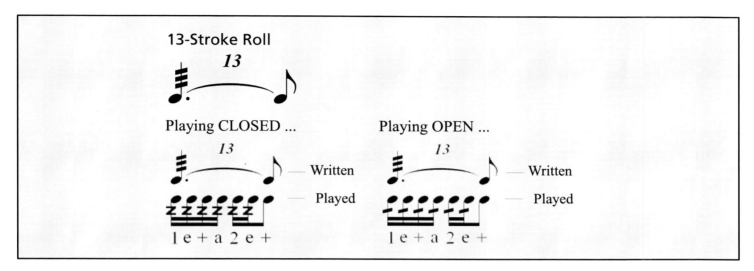

17-Stroke Roll

The 17-stroke roll is executed by playing eight sets of buzz or double strokes followed by a single hit. When playing "open" (with double strokes), there are a total of 17 strokes played on the drumhead, giving the 17-stroke roll its name.

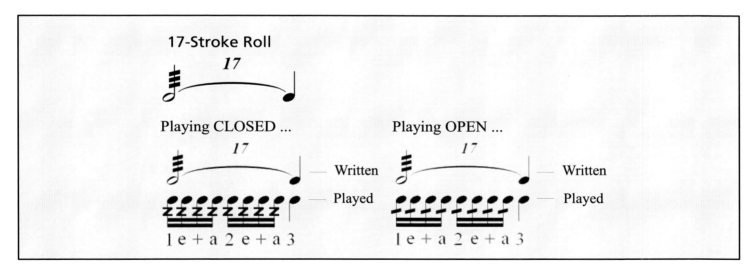

DIRECTIONS: Draw the bar lines where they belong, and then play each line.

✔ Add the 13-stroke roll and 17-stroke roll to the Warm-Up Chart (p.4)

The 13-Stroke Roll & 17-Stroke Roll 2

DIRECTIONS: For each measure below, complete the top number of the time signature, and then write the letter of the measure on the right that is counted the same as the measure on the left. The first one is done for you.

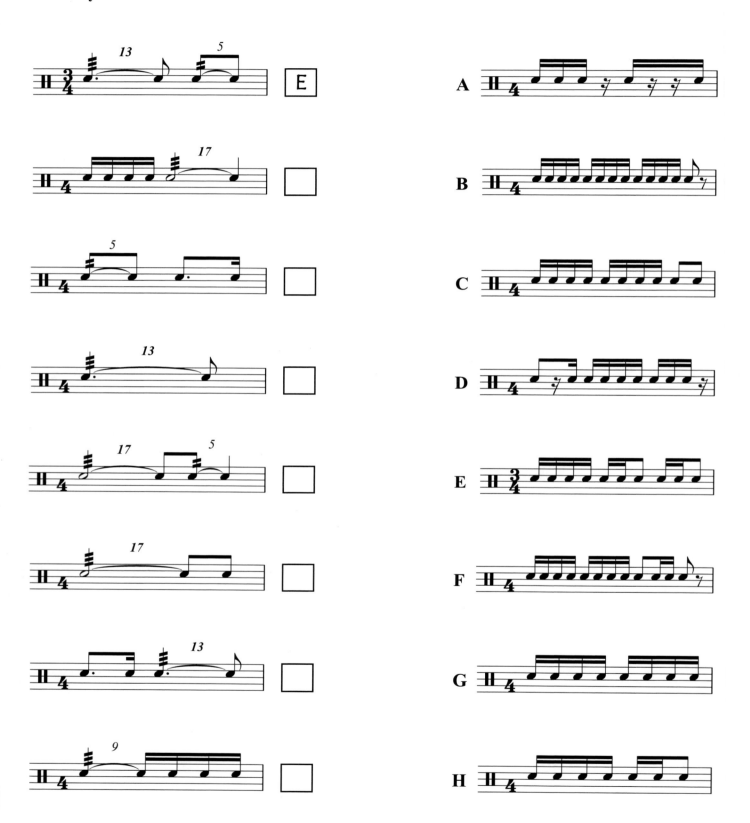

Buy books and study them. "Well, I can't read music." Learn how. It's simple. —Rich Russo, Andrew W.K.

Eighth-Note Triplets 1

Though not used as often as the other notes we've learned so far, reading and playing triplets is still an essential skill for any serious musician/drummer. Triplets can provide a different feel to a groove or a sense of time change. Solid triplets make for solid, impressive drumming.

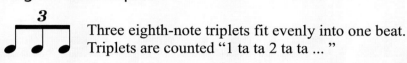

Eighth-Note Triplet

Three eighth-note triplets fit evenly into one beat.
Triplets are counted "1 ta ta 2 ta ta … "

Timing Eighth-Note Triplets
Three eighth-note triplets take up the same amount of time as one quarter note. It's important to play them evenly spaced and not rushed. Getting used to the timing of the triplet can be difficult because of the odd number of notes that fit into one count. Great timing will come with practice.

DIRECTIONS: Write the beat numbers in the boxes below the notes, and then play each line.

Eighth-Note Triplets 2

PART A

DIRECTIONS: Write the appropriate note above each number, and the appropriate rest to match each "x." The first one is done for you.

1 ta ta 2 + | 1 ta ta 2 ta ta | x + 2 ta ta | 1 + 2

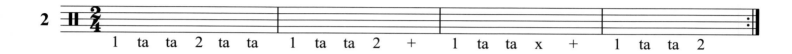

1 ta ta 2 ta ta | 1 ta ta 2 + | 1 ta ta x + | 1 ta ta 2

1 ta ta x | 1 + 2 ta ta | x 2 e + | 1 ta ta x

PART B

DIRECTIONS: Beam the stems on the notes below so you have the correct number of beats in each measure, and then write the beat number below each note.*

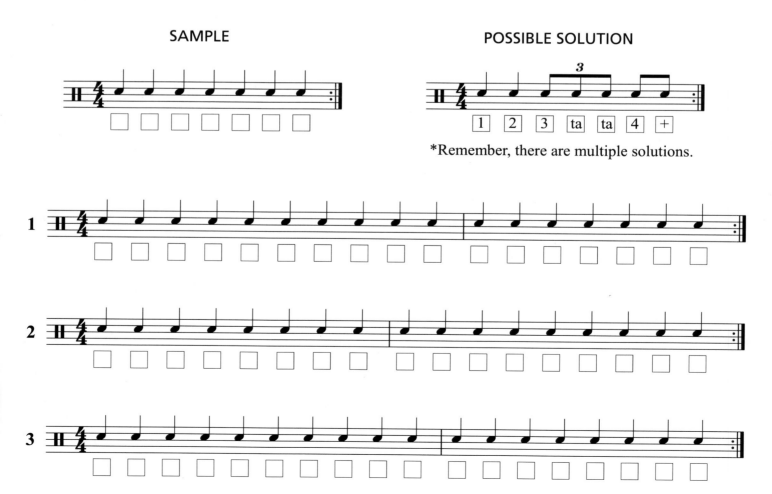

SAMPLE

POSSIBLE SOLUTION

1 | 2 | 3 | ta | ta | 4 | +

*Remember, there are multiple solutions.

Sixteenth-Note Triplets 1

Another type of triplet is the sixteenth-note triplet. Remember that reading and playing triplets is an essential skill for any serious musician/drummer. Triplets can provide a different feel to a groove or a sense of time change. Solid triplets make for solid, impressive drumming.

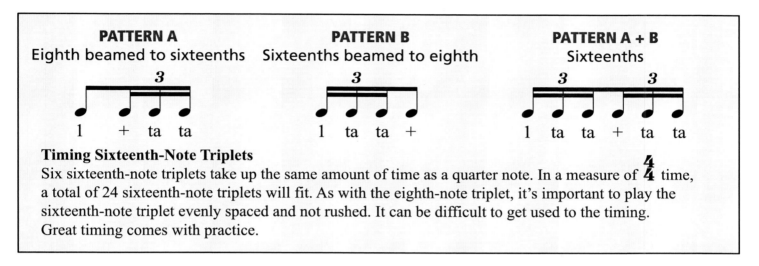

PATTERN A
Eighth beamed to sixteenths

PATTERN B
Sixteenths beamed to eighth

PATTERN A + B
Sixteenths

Timing Sixteenth-Note Triplets

Six sixteenth-note triplets take up the same amount of time as a quarter note. In a measure of $\frac{4}{4}$ time, a total of 24 sixteenth-note triplets will fit. As with the eighth-note triplet, it's important to play the sixteenth-note triplet evenly spaced and not rushed. It can be difficult to get used to the timing. Great timing comes with practice.

DIRECTIONS: Write the beat numbers in the boxes below the notes, and then play each line.

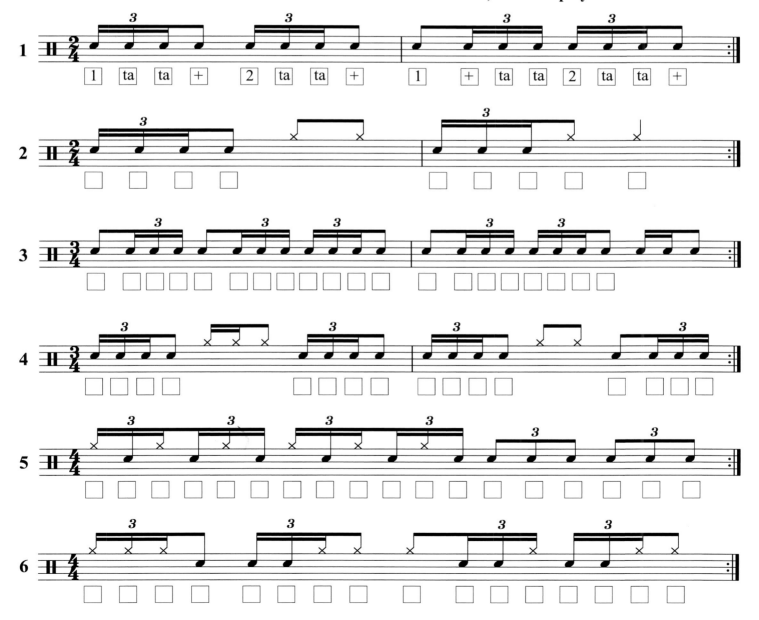

Sixteenth-Note Triplets 2

PART A

DIRECTIONS: Write the appropriate note above each number, and the appropriate rest to match each "x." The first one is done for you.

1   1   +   ta   ta   2   +   ta   ta   1   ta   ta   +   2   +   1   ta   ta   +   ta   ta   2   +   1   ta   ta   +   2

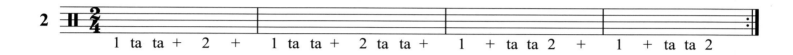

2   1   ta   ta   +   2   +   1   ta   ta   +   2   ta   ta   +   1   +   ta   ta   2   +   1   +   ta   ta   2

3   1   +   2   ta   ta   +   ta   ta   x   +   2   ta   ta   +   x   +   2   +   ta   ta   x   +   a   2

PART B

DIRECTIONS: Beam the stems on the notes below so you have the correct number of beats in each measure, and then write the beat number below each note.*

SAMPLE   POSSIBLE SOLUTION

1   +   ta   ta   2   e   +

*Remember, there are multiple solutions.

The Seven-Stroke Roll 1

The seven-stroke roll is executed by playing three sets of buzz or double strokes followed by a single hit.
When playing "open" (with double strokes), there are a total of seven strokes played on the drumhead,
giving the seven-stroke roll its name.

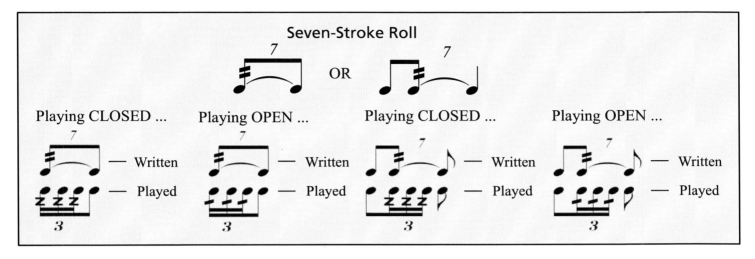

DIRECTIONS: Write the appropriate beat numbers in the boxes below, and then play each line.
Be sure to note the time signature of each line. The first one is done for you.

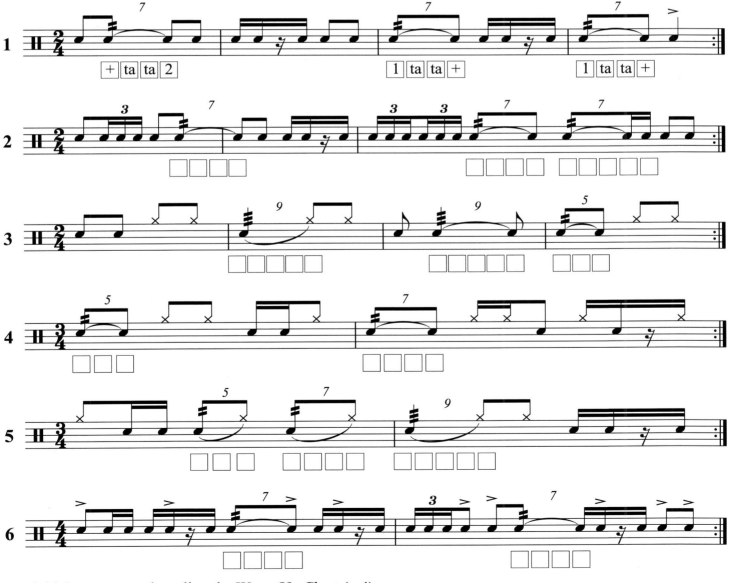

✔ Add the seven-stroke roll to the Warm-Up Chart (p.4)

The Seven-Stroke Roll 2

DIRECTIONS: For each measure below, complete the top number of the time signature, and then write the letter of the measure on the right that is counted the same as the measure on the left. The first one is done for you.

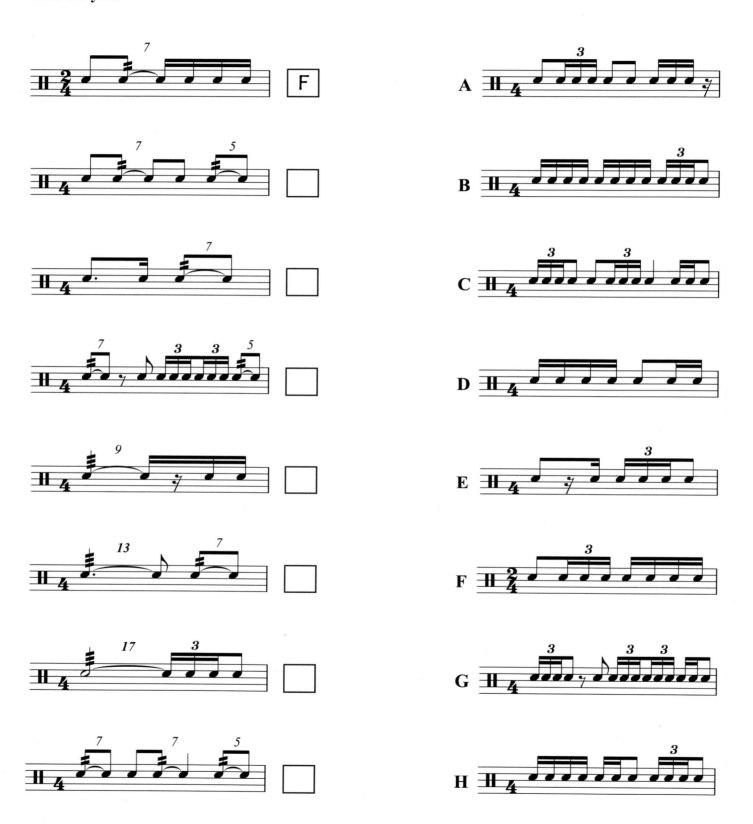

Whatever you decide to play, and hopefully every time you decide to play, own it. —Bryan Hitt, REO Speedwagon

Check-Up

PART A

DIRECTIONS: On the lines below, write the total number of beats for each line.
The first one is done for you.

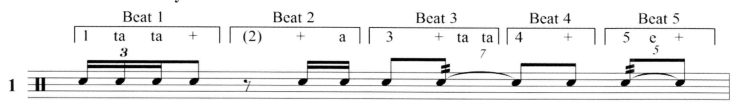

NUMBER OF BEATS: Line 1 ___5___   Line 2 _____   Line 3 _____   Line 4 _____

PART B

DIRECTIONS: In the boxes below, write the selection from the right that will complete the
measure on the left. In other words, match the selections that together will add up to four beats.

The Flam 1

In drumming, changing the stroke style gives the drummer a selection of sounds to pick from, even while playing on one surface. One important stroke is the grace stroke, which is played slightly ahead of a main stroke. The *flam*, another rudiment defined by the Percussive Arts Society, is executed by playing a soft grace stroke starting at about two inches above the drumhead followed by a main stroke. It's important that the grace stroke and main stroke work together to make one distinct sound rather than two distinguishable hits.

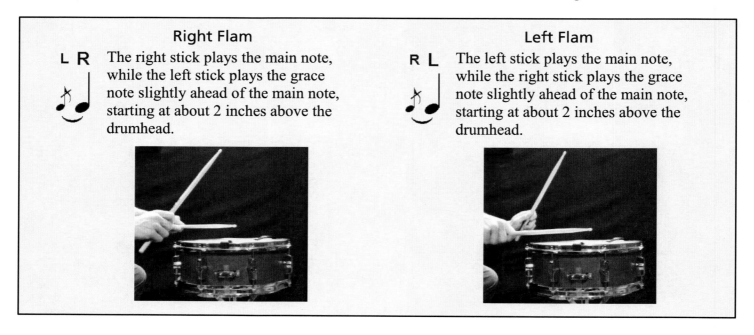

Right Flam
The right stick plays the main note, while the left stick plays the grace note slightly ahead of the main note, starting at about 2 inches above the drumhead.

Left Flam
The left stick plays the main note, while the right stick plays the grace note slightly ahead of the main note, starting at about 2 inches above the drumhead.

DIRECTIONS: Write the beat number below each note, and then play each line (see #1).

✔ Add the flam to the Warm-Up Chart (p.4)

The Flam 2

PART A

DIRECTIONS: Add grace notes below to make flams. Be sure to put them in places where they will make the rhythm sound interesting, and then play each line.

PART B

DIRECTIONS: Beam the stems on the notes below so you have the correct number of beats in each measure, add grace notes to make flams, and write the appropriate beat numbers in the boxes.*

SAMPLE   POSSIBLE SOLUTION

*Remember, there are multiple solutions.

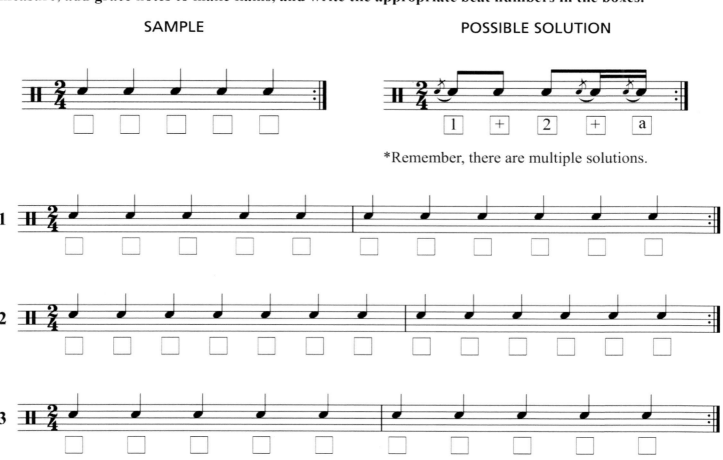

The fun of becoming a great drummer is ... navigating the journey of learning, studying, and practicing. —Donny Gruendler, Author

The Drag 1

Another rudiment defined by the Percussive Arts Society is the drag (or *3-stroke ruff*), which is executed similarly to the *flam* (see p.64) except that the *drag* consists of two soft grace strokes followed by a louder main stroke. The hands should be positioned the same as for the flam (see p.64).

Right Drag	Left Drag
The right stick plays the main note, while the left stick plays two grace notes slightly ahead of the main note, starting at about 2 inches above the drumhead.	The left stick plays the main note, while the right stick plays two grace notes slightly ahead of the main note, starting at about 2 inches above the drumhead.

DIRECTIONS: Write the beat number below each note, and then play each line (see #1).

✔ Add the drag to the Warm-Up Chart (p.4)

The Drag 2

PART A

DIRECTIONS: Add grace notes below to make drags. Be sure to put them in places where they will make the rhythm sound interesting, and then play each line.

PART B

DIRECTIONS: Beam the stems on the notes below so you have the correct number of beats in each measure, add grace notes to make drags, and write the appropriate beat numbers in the boxes.*

SAMPLE   POSSIBLE SOLUTION

*Remember, there are multiple solutions.

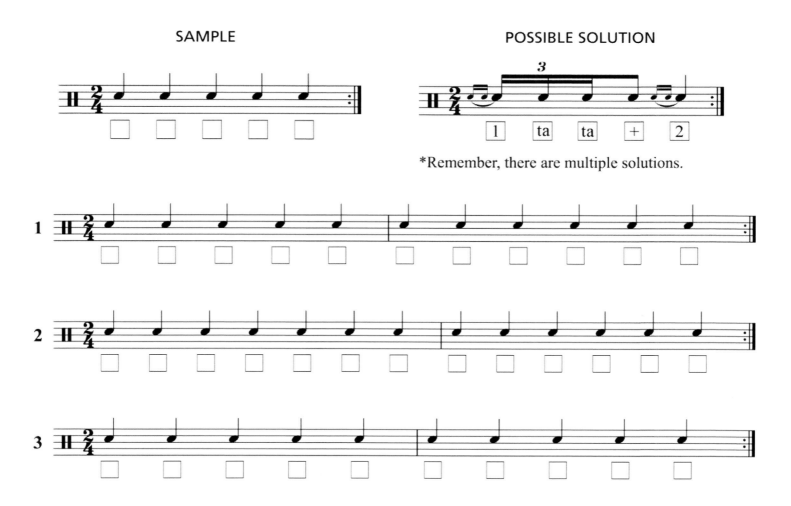

Changes in Tempo

Another way to add interest to a song or rhythm is to change the tempo. There are a number of terms and symbols that direct the reader to change the tempo in a specific way. The three you will learn are *ritardando, accelerando* and the *fermata.*

Ritardando
Ritardando (abbreviated: *rit.*) means to gradually slow down. If there is someone directing the music, it's important to follow his/her cues. Otherwise, the tempo change is up to the player.

Fermata 𝄐
A *fermata* indicates that the player should hold or sustain the note or rest for longer than the note value. It is up to the director or player to determine how long to hold the *fermata.*

Accelerando
Accelerando (abbreviated: *accel.*) means to gradually speed up. If there is someone directing the music, it's important to follow his/her cues. Otherwise, the tempo change is up to the player.

A Tempo
a tempo means to return to the initial tempo of the music.

DIRECTIONS: Play the following piece along with the appropriate dynamics and tempo changes.

Drums Make Sounds

Get as many sounds out of it as possible ... That is done by getting really good expression—hearing different sections of the music that need a different sound. —Ralph Salmins, session drummer

Final Solo

Congratulations! If you've made it this far, you've attained the fundamental knowledge and skills needed to be a successful drummer. You are now ready for your first job, which is to write this book's final solo. Take your time, and think about the rhythms. Don't forget to include time signature indications, tempo changes, and dynamics.

DIRECTIONS: Use the notes, rests, repeats and dynamics you've learned in this book to create the final solo.

Final Test—Part 1

PART A
DIRECTIONS: Match the note on the left with its name on the right.

1. _____   **A.** Whole Note

2. _____   **B.** Sixteenth Note

3. _____   **C.** Quarter Note

4. _____   **D.** Half Note

5. _____   **E.** Eighth Note

PART B
DIRECTIONS: Write out the following dynamic symbols in order from quietest to loudest.

mp   *f*   *p*   *mf*   *ff*   *pp*

6. _____   _____   _____   _____   _____   _____

PART C
DIRECTIONS: Match the symbols on the left with their meaning on the right.

7. _____   **A.** Repeat the previous measure

8. _____ >   **B.** Gradually get softer

9. _____   **C.** Gradually get louder

10. _____   **D.** Indicates to repeat a selection of music

11. _____   **E.** Repeat the two previous measures

12. _____   **F.** Play the note louder than its surrounding notes

13. _____   /   **G.** Indicates the end of a measure

14. _____   **H.** Improvise a selection of music

PART D
DIRECTIONS: Write out the following rests from longest duration to shortest.

15. _____   _____   _____   _____   _____

Final Test—Part 2

PART A

DIRECTIONS: Use the lines of music below to answer questions 1–6.

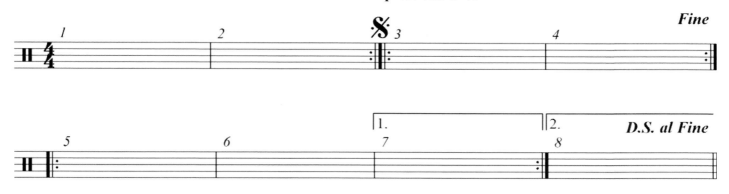

1. After playing measure 2 the first time, which measure is played? _____

2. After playing measure 4 the first time, which measure is played? _____

3. Which measure is played after measure 7? _____

4. After playing measure 6 the second time, which measure is played? _____

5. Which measure is played after measure 8? _____

6. In which measure does the piece end? _____

PART B

DIRECTIONS: Use the lines of music below to answer questions 7–10.

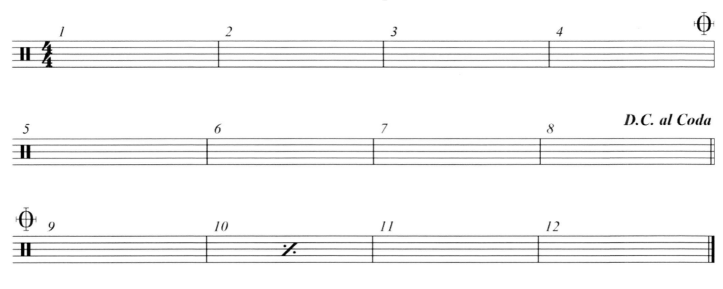

7. Which measure is played after playing measure 8? _____

8. After playing measure 4 the second time, which measure is played? _____

9. Which measure is repeated in measure 10? _____

10. In which measure does the piece end? _____

Final Test—Part 3

PART A

DIRECTIONS: Write the beat number below each note.

PART B

DIRECTIONS: Complete the time signatures for each measure below.

ANSWER SHEETS

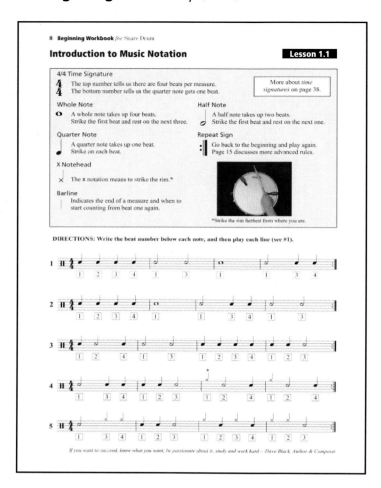

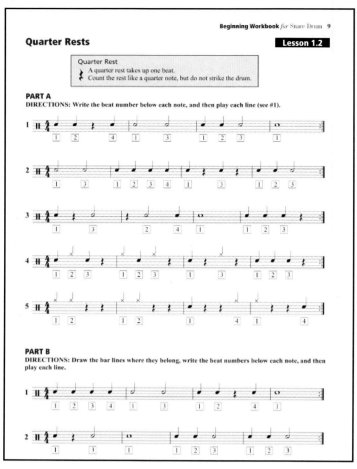

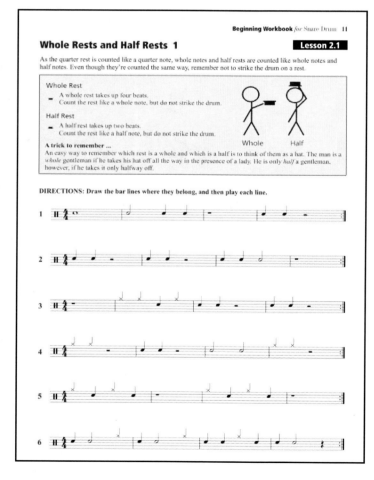

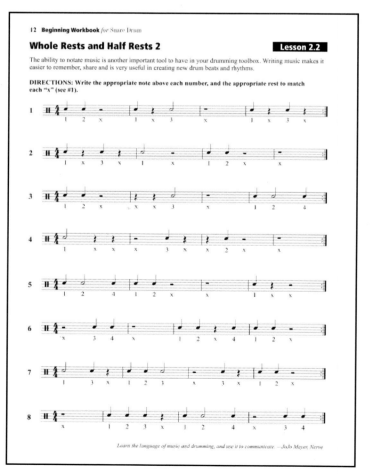

Eighth Notes 1

Lesson 3.1

The eighth note is one of the most commonly played notes in today's music and, as such, is very important. You will find eighth notes at the heart of almost every hit song. Master the eighth note and you are on your way to becoming a successful drummer.

Eighth Note	Eighth Notes—Beamed
An eighth note takes up half a beat (two fit in one beat). They are counted "1 & 2 & 3 & 4 &."	When eighth notes are next to each other, their flags can connect to form a *beam*.

DIRECTIONS: Write the beat number below each note using a "+" sign to represent each "&" and then play each line.

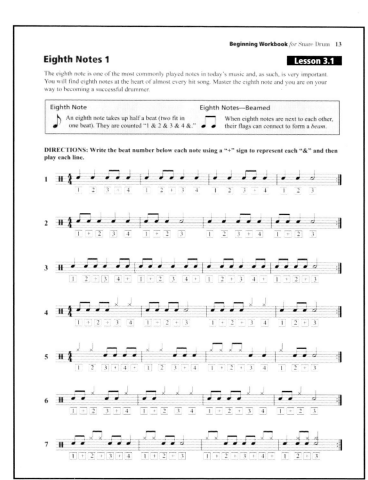

Eighth Notes 2

Lesson 3.2

Which notes should be beamed together?
Most often, notes are beamed together to group them into beats. In other words, all of the notes that make up beat one are beamed together. All of the notes that make up beat two are beamed together. This continues for each beat. However, it is also common to see four eighth notes beamed together, making up two beats. Following a consistent beaming structure makes the music clearer and easier to follow.

PART A
DIRECTIONS: Beam the stems on the notes below so you have the correct number of beats in each measure. Then, write the beat number below each note. There are multiple possibilities for each measure. Be creative!

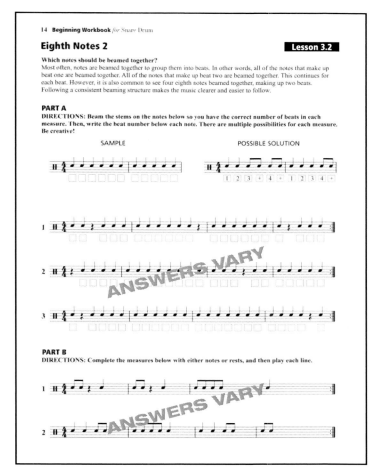

PART B
DIRECTIONS: Complete the measures below with either notes or rests, and then play each line.

Repeats and 1st & 2nd Endings

Lesson 3.3

Repeat Signs
The repeat sign you've used so far is called an *end repeat*. There is another repeat sign called a *start repeat* that looks very similar. It is the mirror image of the *end repeat* with its two dots on the right side (see below).

Start Repeat	End Repeat
Indicates where to start repeating after an *end repeat*. If a *start repeat* is not present, repeat from the beginning of the piece.	Indicates to repeat a selection of music. Once you've repeated the selection, play through the *end repeat* as if it's not there.

DIRECTIONS: Use the following piece to answer the questions below, and then play the piece.

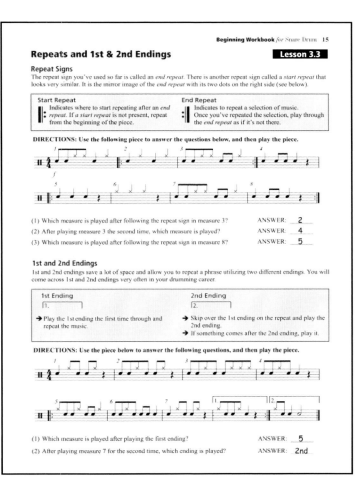

(1) Which measure is played after following the repeat sign in measure 3?   ANSWER: 2

(2) After playing measure 3 the second time, which measure is played?   ANSWER: 4

(3) Which measure is played after following the repeat sign in measure 8?   ANSWER: 5

1st and 2nd Endings
1st and 2nd endings save a lot of space and allow you to repeat a phrase utilizing two different endings. You will come across 1st and 2nd endings very often in your drumming career.

1st Ending	2nd Ending
→ Play the 1st ending the first time through and repeat the music.	→ Skip over the 1st ending on the repeat and play the 2nd ending. → If something comes after the 2nd ending, play it.

DIRECTIONS: Use the piece below to answer the following questions, and then play the piece.

(1) Which measure is played after playing the first ending?   ANSWER: 5

(2) After playing measure 7 for the second time, which ending is played?   ANSWER: 2nd

Dynamics 1

Lesson 3.4

The term *dynamics* refers to how loudly or softly something is sung or played. Dynamics should already be familiar to you, as we use them in our speech. You may talk loudly when you're angry or softly when you want to keep a secret. Dynamics add meaning and interest to music. A dynamic drummer stands out above the rest.

Piano	Forte
p A *piano* marking means to play quietly. Play *piano* until another dynamic is indicated.	*f* A *forte* marking means to play loudly. Play *forte* until another dynamic is indicated.
Crescendo	Decrescendo
Gradually get louder for the notes above the crescendo.	Gradually get softer for the notes above the decrescendo.

Measure Repeat
A *measure repeat* means to repeat the previous measure and then go on. In other words, whatever you just played, play it again.

PART A
DIRECTIONS: Play the following piece along with the appropriate dynamics.

Shank

Turning It Up

PART B
DIRECTIONS: Add dynamics to the following piece to make it more interesting, and then play the piece.

My Dynamics

You should play from your heart, your soul, your instinct. —Dino Campanella, DREDG

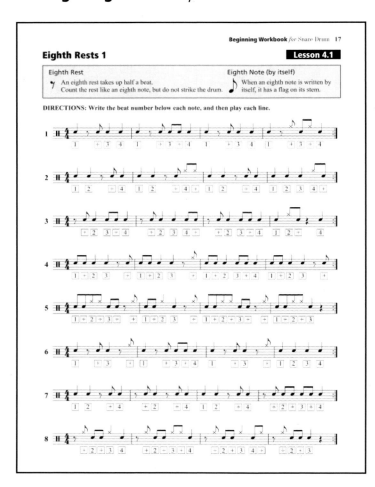

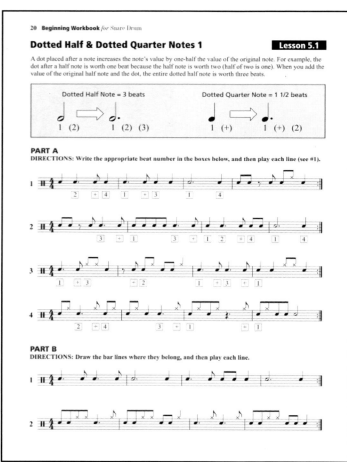

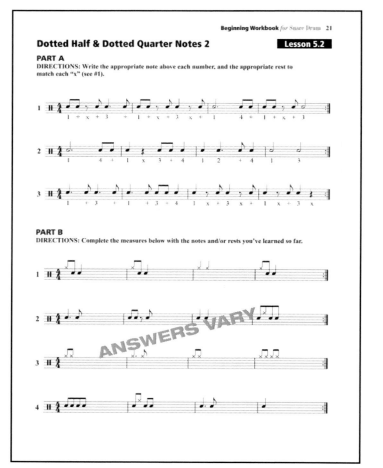

Dynamics 2 **Lesson 5.3**

So far you have learned four dynamic expressions: *piano, forte, crescendo* and *decrescendo.*
The compositions below incorporate two more dynamic expressions: *pianissimo* and *fortissimo.*

Pianissimo	Fortissimo
pp *Pianissimo* means to play very quietly. *Pianissimo* is quieter than *piano.*	**ff** *Fortissimo* means to play very loudly. *Fortissimo* is louder than *forte.*

pp *very quiet*   **p** *quiet*   **f** *loud*   **ff** *very loud*

PART A
DIRECTIONS: Play the following piece along with the appropriate dynamics.

PART B
DIRECTIONS: Add dynamics to the following piece to make it more interesting, and then play the piece.

Dal Segno al Fine **Lesson 5.4**

𝄋 = The sign. Indicates where to go back after a *D.S.*	*Dal Segno (D.S.)* = Go back to *the sign*
D.S. al Fine = Go back to *the sign*	*Fine* = The end

PART A
DIRECTIONS: Use the following piece to answer the questions below, and then play the piece.

Courtside

(1) Which measure is played after playing the second ending?   ANSWER: 9

(2) Which measure is played after playing the first ending?   ANSWER: 13

(3) In which measure does the piece end?   ANSWER: 12

PART B
DIRECTIONS: Add *the sign, D.S. al Fine* and *Fine* to the piece below, and then play the piece.

Most successful musicians didn't win their first audition, and if they all quit the first or second time they were turned down, then we wouldn't have Jimi Hendrix, and we wouldn't have all these great players. —Paulo Baldi, CAKE

Sixteenth Notes **Lesson 6.1**

Every drummer must master the timing and feel of the sixteenth note. The addition of the sixteenth note will greatly expand your rhythmic possibilities. Used in most of today's popular music, the sixteenth note is another essential tool to add to your drumming "toolbox."

Sixteenth Note	Sixteenth Notes Beamed
A sixteenth note takes up a quarter (1/4) of a beat. They are counted "1 e & a 2 e & a ..." Four sixteenth notes take up the same amount of time as a quarter note.	When sixteenth notes are next to each other, their flags can connect to form two *beams.*

PART A
DIRECTIONS: Write the appropriate beat number in the boxes below, and then play each line (see #1).

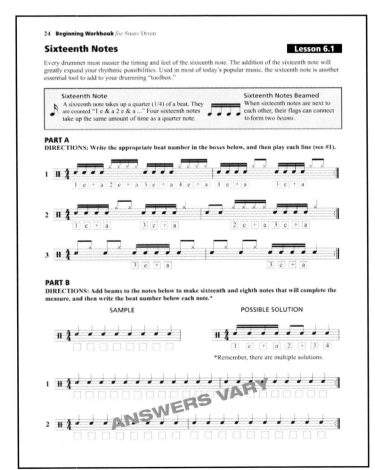

PART B
DIRECTIONS: Add beams to the notes below to make sixteenth and eighth notes that will complete the measure, and then write the beat number below each note.*

SAMPLE   POSSIBLE SOLUTION

*Remember, there are multiple solutions.

Sixteenth Notes—Duet **Lesson 6.2**

DIRECTIONS: Fill in the missing measures to complete the duet, and then add dynamics to the piece.

Your Half

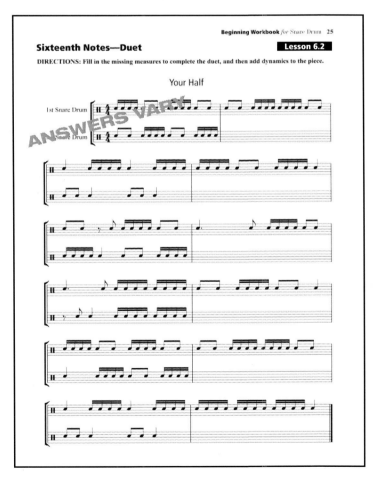

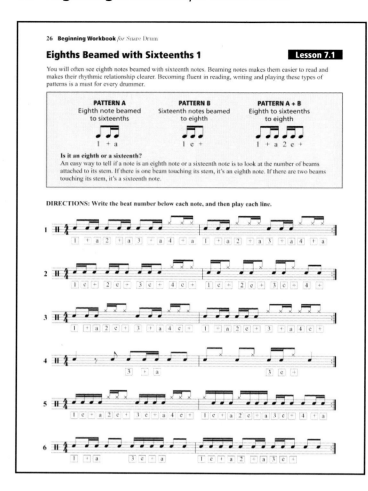

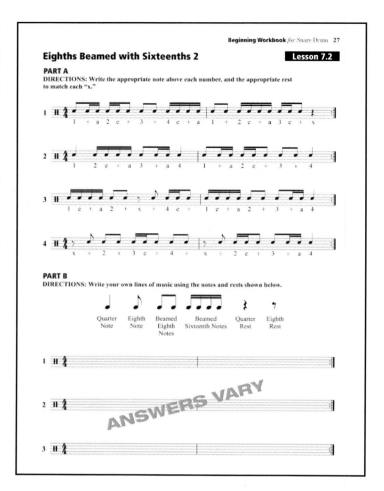

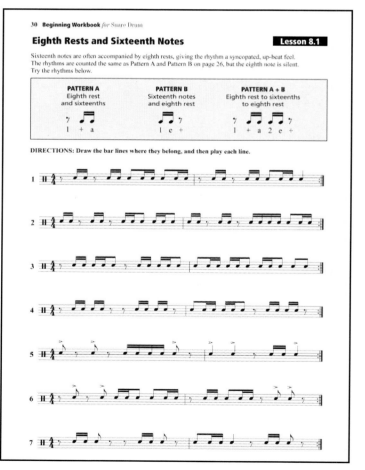

Sixteenth Rests

Lesson 8.3

Sixteenth Rest
A sixteenth rest takes up a quarter (1/4) of a beat. Count the rest like a sixteenth note, but do not strike the drum.

Sixteenth Note
When a sixteenth note is written by itself, it includes two flags on its stem.

PART A
DIRECTIONS: Write the appropriate beat number in the boxes below, and then play each line.

PART B
DIRECTIONS: Add beams and rests to the notes below to make sixteenth and eighth notes/rests that will complete the measure, and then write the beat number below each note.*

SAMPLE

POSSIBLE SOLUTION

*Remember, there are multiple solutions.

ANSWERS VARY

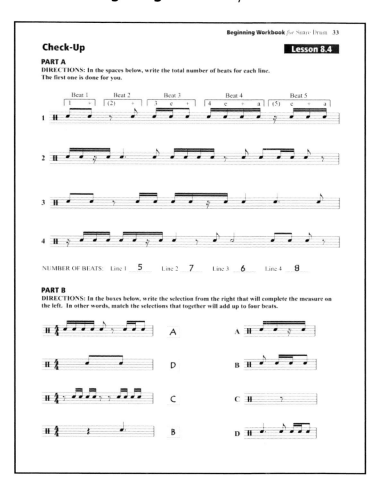

Check-Up

Lesson 8.4

PART A
DIRECTIONS: In the spaces below, write the total number of beats for each line. The first one is done for you.

Beat 1   Beat 2   Beat 3   Beat 4   Beat 5

NUMBER OF BEATS: Line 1 5   Line 2 7   Line 3 6   Line 4 8

PART B
DIRECTIONS: In the boxes below, write the selection from the right that will complete the measure on the left. In other words, match the selections that together will add up to four beats.

A   A
D   B
C   C
B   D

Da Capo al Coda

Lesson 8.5

⊕ = Coda sign

D.C. al Coda = Go back to the beginning and play to the coda sign (⊕). Once you reach the first coda sign, skip ahead to the second coda sign, and play from there.

Da Capo (D.C.) = Go back to the beginning

2 Two-measure repeat. When you see ⫽ this, repeat the previous two measures.

PART A
DIRECTIONS: Use the piece below to answer the questions that follow, and then play the piece.

Shank

D.C. al Coda

(4) Which measure is played after playing measure 6? ANSWER: 1
(5) Which measure is played after playing measure 4 the second time? ANSWER: 7
(6) In which measure does the piece end? ANSWER: 8

PART B
DIRECTIONS: Add *coda* signs and *D.C. al Coda* to the piece below, and then play the piece.

ANSWERS VARY

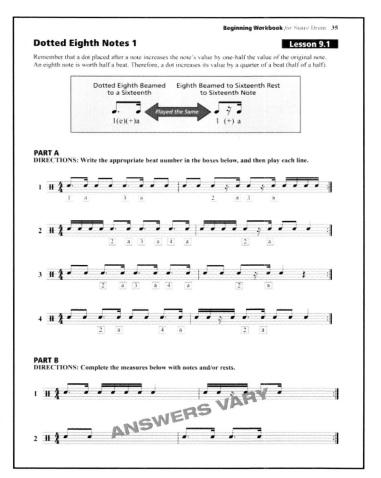

Dotted Eighth Notes 1

Lesson 9.1

Remember that a dot placed after a note increases the note's value by one-half the value of the original note. An eighth note is worth half a beat. Therefore, a dot increases its value by a quarter of a beat (half of a half).

Dotted Eighth Beamed to a Sixteenth

Played the Same

Eighth Beamed to Sixteenth Rest to Sixteenth Note

1 (e) (+) a   1 (+) a

PART A
DIRECTIONS: Write the appropriate beat number in the boxes below, and then play each line.

PART B
DIRECTIONS: Complete the measures below with notes and/or rests.

ANSWERS VARY

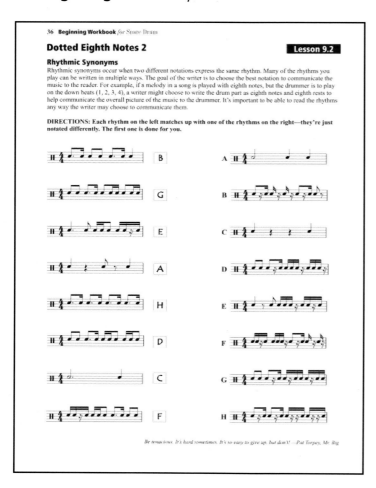

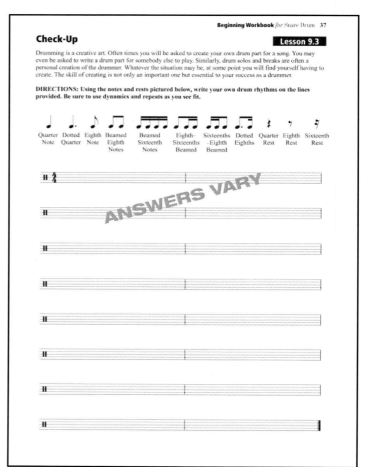

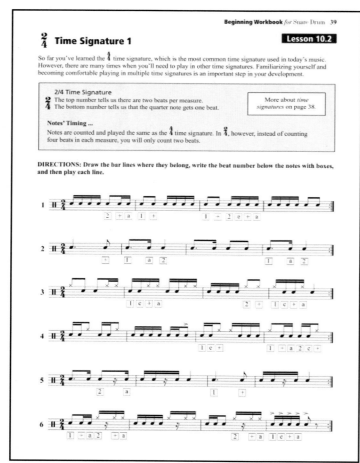

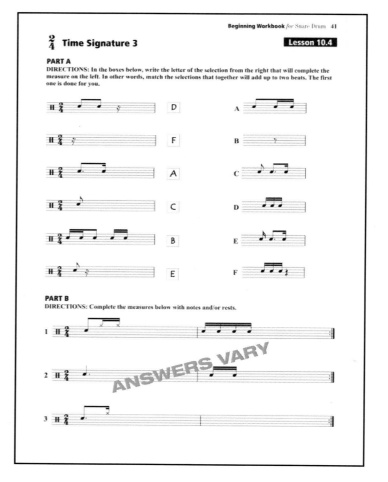

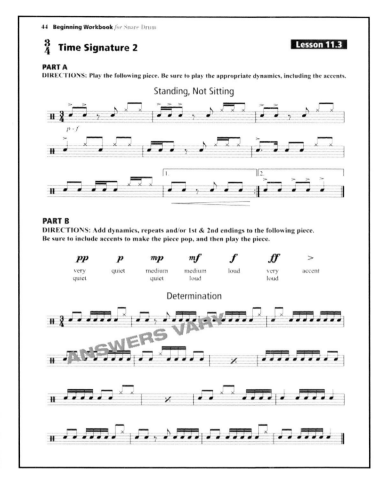

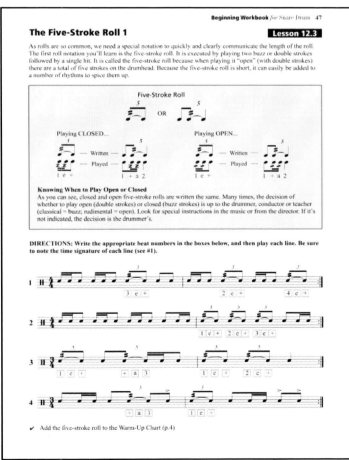

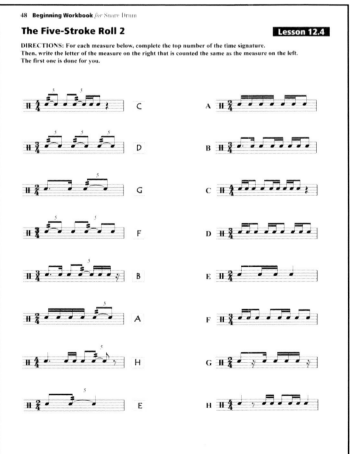

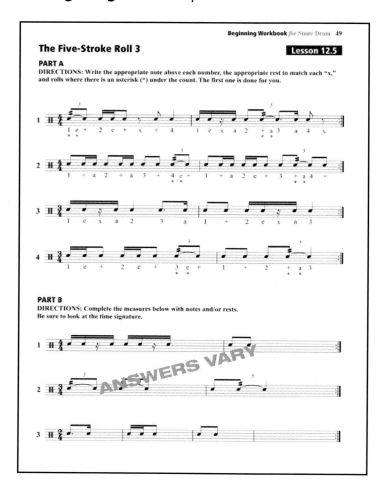

The Five-Stroke Roll 3   **Lesson 12.5**

PART A
DIRECTIONS: Write the appropriate note above each number, the appropriate rest to match each "x," and rolls where there is an asterisk (*) under the count. The first one is done for you.

PART B
DIRECTIONS: Complete the measures below with notes and/or rests. Be sure to look at the time signature.

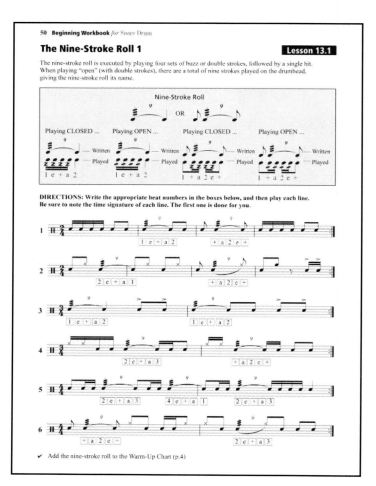

The Nine-Stroke Roll 1   **Lesson 13.1**

The nine-stroke roll is executed by playing four sets of buzz or double strokes, followed by a single hit. When playing "open" (with double strokes), there are a total of nine strokes played on the drumhead, giving the nine-stroke roll its name.

DIRECTIONS: Write the appropriate beat numbers in the boxes below, and then play each line. Be sure to note the time signature of each line. The first one is done for you.

✔ Add the nine-stroke roll to the Warm-Up Chart (p.4)

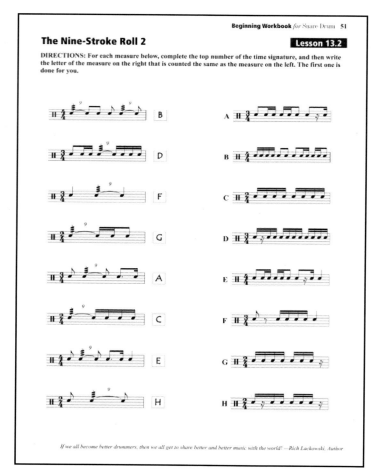

The Nine-Stroke Roll 2   **Lesson 13.2**

DIRECTIONS: For each measure below, complete the top number of the time signature, and then write the letter of the measure on the right that is counted the same as the measure on the left. The first one is done for you.

If we all become better drummers, then we all get to share better and better music with the world! —Rich Lackowski, Author

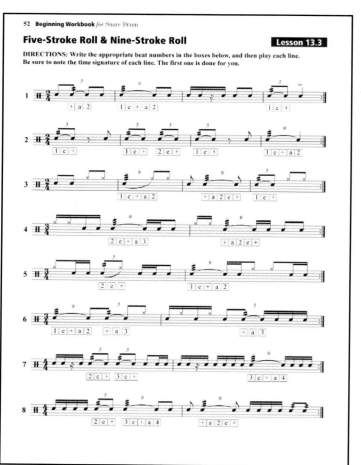

Five-Stroke Roll & Nine-Stroke Roll   **Lesson 13.3**

DIRECTIONS: Write the appropriate beat numbers in the boxes below, and then play each line. Be sure to note the time signature of each line. The first one is done for you.

Check-Up

Continue practicing your writing and creative skills by writing six rhythms below. Try not to rush through this. Think about the rhythms by first sounding them out in your head, and by tapping them out before and after you've written them. The more you create, the easier it will become. A drummer that can create great rhythms is an asset to any band.

DIRECTIONS: Write your own lines of music using any of the notes, rests and/or rolls you've learned so far. Take your time, and be creative!

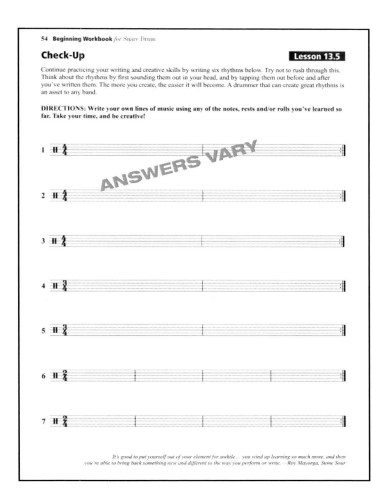

It's good to put yourself out of your element for awhile ... you wind up learning so much more, and then you're able to bring back something new and different to the way you perform or write. — Roy Mayorga, Stone Sour

The 13-Stroke Roll & 17-Stroke Roll 1

13-Stroke Roll

The 13-stroke roll is executed by playing six sets of buzz or double strokes followed by a single hit. When playing "open" (with double strokes), there are a total of 13 strokes played on the drumhead, giving the 13-stroke roll its name.

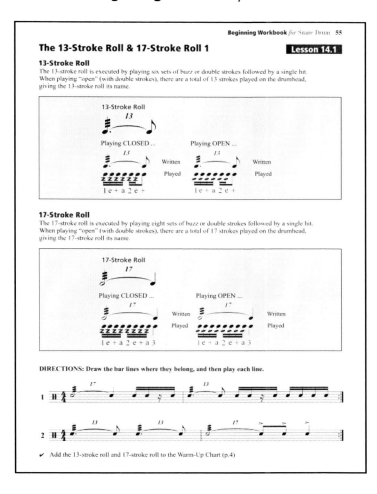

17-Stroke Roll

The 17-stroke roll is executed by playing eight sets of buzz or double strokes followed by a single hit. When playing "open" (with double strokes), there are a total of 17 strokes played on the drumhead, giving the 17-stroke roll its name.

DIRECTIONS: Draw the bar lines where they belong, and then play each line.

✔ Add the 13-stroke roll and 17-stroke roll to the Warm-Up Chart (p.4)

The 13-Stroke Roll & 17-Stroke Roll 2

DIRECTIONS: For each measure below, complete the top number of the time signature, and then write the letter of the measure on the right that is counted the same as the measure on the left. The first one is done for you.

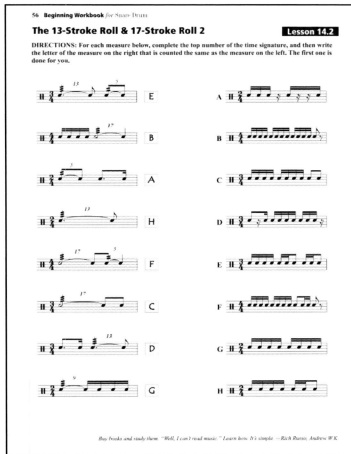

Buy books and study them. "Well, I can't read music." Learn how. It's simple. —Rich Russo, Andrew W.K.

Eighth-Note Triplets 1

Though not used as often as the other notes we've learned so far, reading and playing triplets is still an essential skill for any serious musician/drummer. Triplets can provide a different feel to a groove or a sense of time change. Solid triplets make for solid, impressive drumming.

Eighth-Note Triplet

Three eighth-note triplets fit evenly into one beat. Triplets are counted "1 ta ta 2 ta ta ... "

Timing Eighth-Note Triplets

Three eighth-note triplets take up the same amount of time as one quarter note. It's important to play them evenly spaced and not rushed. Getting used to the timing of the triplet can be difficult because of the odd number of notes that fit into one count. Great timing will come with practice.

DIRECTIONS: Write the beat numbers in the boxes below the notes, and then play each line.

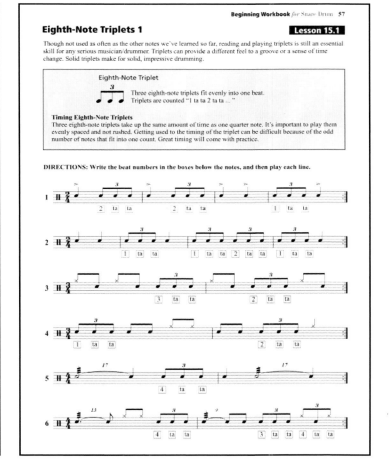

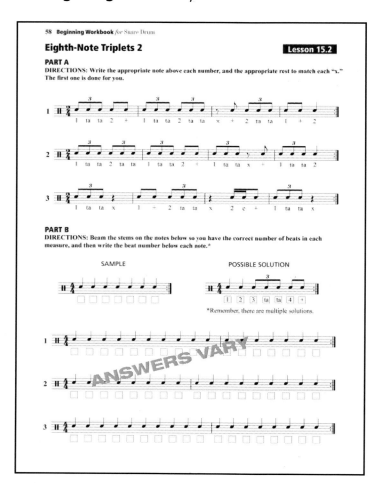

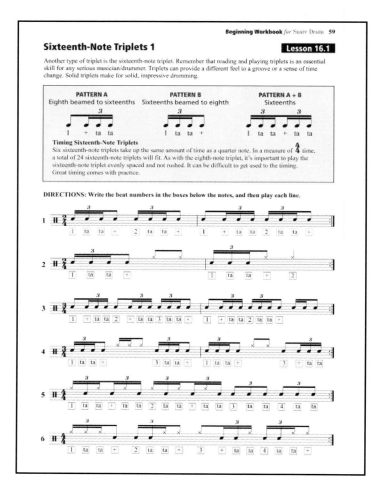

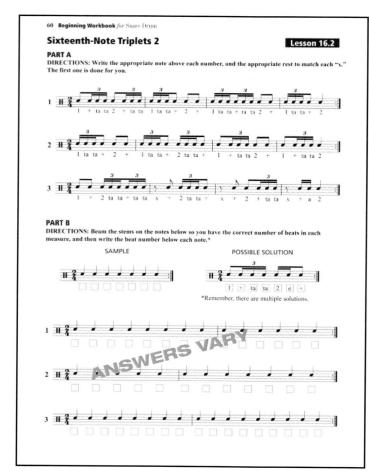

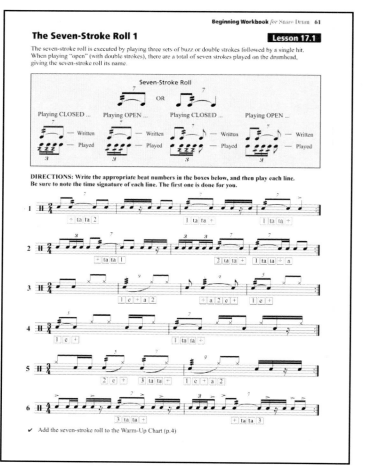

The Seven-Stroke Roll 2

Lesson 17.2

DIRECTIONS: For each measure below, complete the top number of the time signature, and then write the letter of the measure on the right that is counted the same as the measure on the left. The first one is done for you.

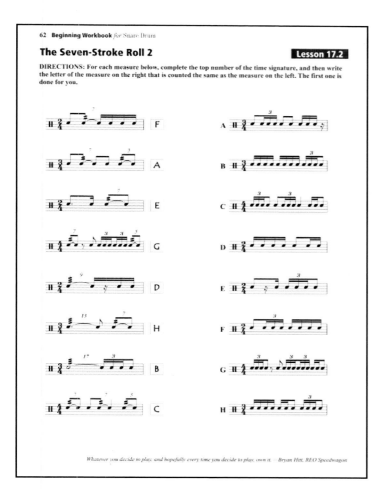

Check-Up

Lesson 17.3

PART A
DIRECTIONS: On the lines below, write the total number of beats for each line. The first one is done for you.

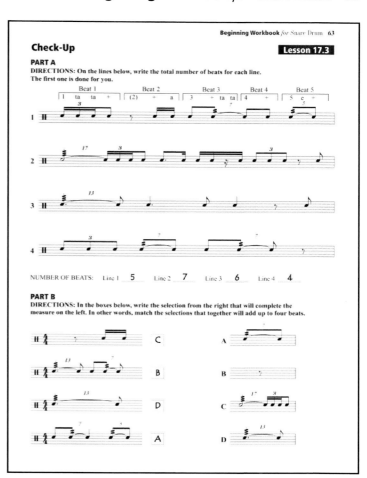

NUMBER OF BEATS: Line 1 **5**   Line 2 **7**   Line 3 **6**   Line 4 **4**

PART B
DIRECTIONS: In the boxes below, write the selection from the right that will complete the measure on the left. In other words, match the selections that together will add up to four beats.

The Flam 1

Lesson 18.1

In drumming, changing the stroke style gives the drummer a selection of sounds to pick from, even while playing on one surface. One important stroke is the grace stroke, which is played slightly ahead of a main stroke. The *flam*, another rudiment defined by the Percussive Arts Society, is executed by playing a soft grace stroke starting at about two inches above the drumhead followed by a main stroke. It's important that the grace stroke and main stroke work together to make one distinct sound rather than two distinguishable hits.

DIRECTIONS: Write the beat number below each note, and then play each line (see #1).

✔ Add the flam to the Warm-Up Chart (p.4)

The Flam 2

Lesson 18.2

PART A
DIRECTIONS: Add grace notes below to make flams. Be sure to put them in places where they will make the rhythm sound interesting, and then play each line.

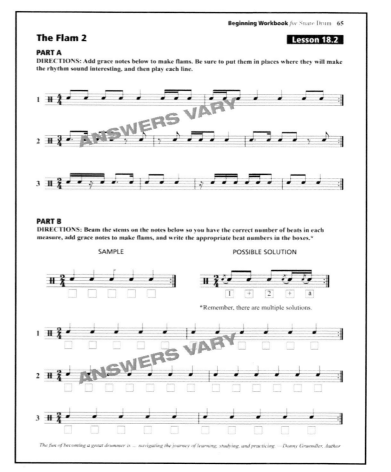

PART B
DIRECTIONS: Beam the stems on the notes below so you have the correct number of beats in each measure, add grace notes to make flams, and write the appropriate beat numbers in the boxes.*

*Remember, there are multiple solutions.

The Drag 1 | Lesson 19.1

Another rudiment defined by the Percussive Arts Society is the *drag* (or *3-stroke ruff*), which is executed similarly to the *flam* (see p.64) except that the *drag* consists of two soft grace strokes followed by a louder main stroke. The hands should be positioned the same as for the flam (see p.64).

DIRECTIONS: Write the beat number below each note, and then play each line (see #1).

✔ Add the drag to the Warm-Up Chart (p.4)

The Drag 2 | Lesson 19.2

PART A
DIRECTIONS: Add grace notes below to make drags. Be sure to put them in places where they will make the rhythm sound interesting, and then play each line.

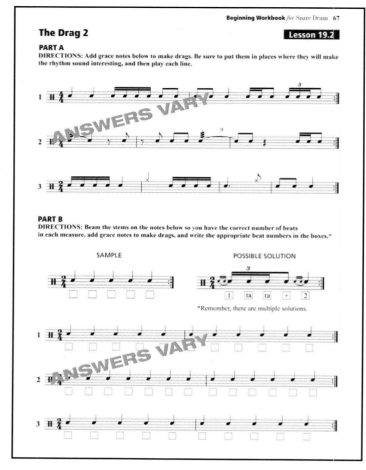

PART B
DIRECTIONS: Beam the stems on the notes below so you have the correct number of beats in each measure, add grace notes to make drags, and write the appropriate beat numbers in the boxes.*

SAMPLE   POSSIBLE SOLUTION

*Remember, there are multiple solutions.

Final Solo | Lesson 20.1

Congratulations! If you've made it this far, you've attained the fundamental knowledge and skills needed to be a successful drummer. You are now ready for your first job, which is to write this book's final solo. Take your time, and think about the rhythms. Don't forget to include time signature indications, tempo changes, and dynamics.

DIRECTIONS: Use the notes, rests, repeats and dynamics you've learned in this book to create the final solo.

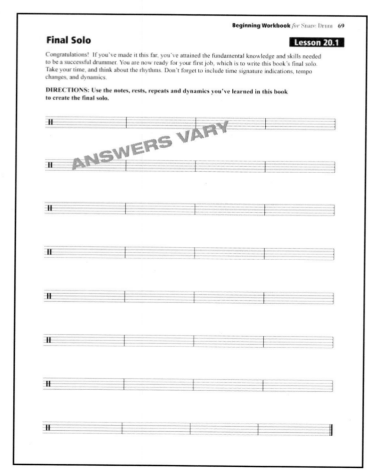

Final Test—Part 1 | Lesson 20.2

PART A
DIRECTIONS: Match the note on the left with its name on the right.

1. _C_   **A.** Whole Note

2. _A_   **B.** Sixteenth-Note

3. _E_   **C.** Quarter Note

4. _B_   **D.** Half Note

5. _D_   **E.** Eighth-Note

PART B
DIRECTIONS: Write out the following dynamic symbols in order from quietest to loudest.

mp   *f*   *p*   *mf*   *ff*   *pp*

6. *pp*   *p*   *mp*   *mf*   *f*   *ff*

PART C
DIRECTIONS: Match the symbols on the left with their meaning on the right.

7. _D_   **A.** Repeat the previous measure

8. _F_   **B.** Gradually get softer

9. _A_   **C.** Gradually get louder

10. _G_   **D.** Indicates to repeat a selection of music

11. _C_   **E.** Repeat the two previous measures

12. _B_   **F.** Play the note louder than its surrounding notes

13. _H_   **G.** Indicates the end of a measure

14. _E_   **H.** Improvise a selection of music

PART D
DIRECTIONS: Write out the following rests from longest duration to shortest.

15.

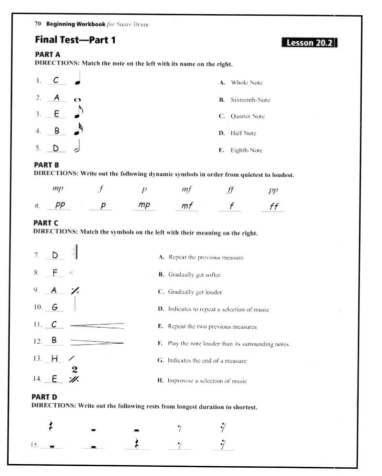